"Marina and Marina's book offers over three decades of practical experience and innovative research toward centralizing human rights within criminal justice and policing specifically. *Human Rights Policing: Reimagining Law Enforcement in the 21st Century* could not be more salient in these extraordinary times. While many of us imagine impending crisis on a global scale, this book—through tremendous insight, experience and intellectual humility—offer ethical ways forward for policing and the education of future practitioners. I cannot personally imagine a more innovative or realist approach to the complex condition of modern policing with the baggage of colonialist histories during this historic moment of growing social disparities. Both Peter and Pedro's voices ring out clearly throughout this text. One voice has the insight and articulation of well-travelled ethnographer while the other adds decades of policing experience, respectively. This book offers insightful re-conceptualizations for policing and education in criminal justice/criminology that few (if any) books currently contain."

Edward LW Green, Roosevelt University in Chicago, IL

"Professor Marina and retired N.O.P.D Lieutenant Pedro Marina bring a fresh, innovative, and exciting perspective on human rights and policing. Their book offers a paradigm shift away from the 'This is the way we have always done it,' mentality currently keeping police agencies from evolving. This book is a must-read for police chiefs and law enforcement executives looking for a way to jump-start their agencies' community engagement philosophy and improve understanding of the role human rights plays in policing."

Ron Camacho, Chief of the Chambersburg Pennsylvania Police Department

"*Human Rights Policing* is a collaboration between a retired lieutenant from the New Orleans Police Department, with 30 years of experience in law enforcement, and an academic sociologist known for his longstanding commitment to challenging the systemic issues that have plagued US policing. Their shared mission is to put forward a new model of policing that they call 'Human Rights Policing', which is based upon the United Nations' definition of human rights, which includes the right to life, liberty, security of person, freedom from arbitrary arrest, detention, and many other protections. Written in an engaging and accessible style, with the use of real-life examples, this book provides a practical guide for the implementation of Human Rights Policing. While it will undoubtedly prove to be essential reading for all those working in law enforcement, it also functions as a useful and thought-provoking contribution to the debate on the future of policing in this country."

Jayne Mooney, John Jay College of Criminal Justice, City University of New York

Human Rights Policing

Relying on intense ethnographic research and extensive experiences teaching human rights policing to police officers, this book teaches law enforcement professionals how to apply human rights to their everyday interactions with community members. The data collected throughout this research process offers the reader first-hand accounts of police officers addressing the most important human rights as they relate to policing, telling stories of using their human agency while on the job, and providing insights into their discussions with community members on human rights, among other important topics.

Human rights remain a relatively new concept in human civilization, but one largely unrealized at this point in history. Can police officers serve as the harbingers of human rights in a world that desperately needs it? We say yes. It starts with applying human rights to police work. But this book does more than teach police officers how to apply human rights to their careers. It reimagines the institution of law enforcement as we push toward the later stages of modernity. Refusing to tell readers what to think, this book provides the intellectual tools on how to think about policing in new and creative ways. It seeks to bring out the readers' full creative potential as law enforcement agents, police officers, and criminal justice professionals and activists.

This book advances new ideas throughout each chapter on how to make human rights policing a reality. The ideas in each chapter build on each other, offering a small piece of the puzzle and all the steps necessary to advance the goals of human rights policing. The book (1) analyzes the United Nations Declaration of Human Rights and how it applies to policing, (2) develops a three-fold typology called "Human Rights Policing Social Interactions," (3) discusses the relationship between the use of power and human rights, (4) explains the power of human agency to transcend the ordinary, (5) uncovers the creation of folk devils that threaten human rights, (6) describes how to use the sociological imagination to understand community members, (7) reveals the importance of storytelling to see the world from the actor's point of view, (8) discusses the double consciousness and the creation of the "other," (9) describes what we call "soulful policing" and engaging with the community—Chicago style, and (10) provides social policy suggestions at both the national level and local policing level.

This book will challenge the reader in fascinating and highly surprising ways to think about, and, further, to reimagine policing as we push toward the future. It will appeal to professionals at all levels of law enforcement, and will be useful in programs offering degrees and/or certificates to students of criminal justice.

Peter Marina holds a Ph.D. in sociology from The New School for Social Research in Manhattan, serves as Associate Professor of Sociology & Criminal Justice, and is author of *Down and Out in New Orleans* with Columbia University Press.

Pedro Marina holds a Bachelor's of Arts in Sociology at the University of New Orleans and is a retired police lieutenant from the New Orleans Police Department with 30 years of law enforcement experience in the Big Easy.

Routledge Series on Practical and Evidence-Based Policing

Books in the Routledge Series on Practical and Evidence-Based Policing disseminate knowledge and provide practical tools for law enforcement leaders and personnel to protect and serve the public and reduce crime. With an aim to bridge the "translation gap" between frontline policing and academic research, books in this series apply sound scientific methods as well as practical experience to make everyday police work safer and smarter. These books are an invaluable resource for police practitioners, academic researchers, public policymakers, and students in law enforcement and criminology programs to guide best practices in all aspects of policing.

Police Misconduct Complaint Investigations Manual, 2nd Edition
Barbara Attard & Kathryn Olson

Police and YOUth
Everette B. Penn & Shannon A. Davenport

Twenty-One Mental Models for Policing
A Framework for Using Data and Research for Overcoming Cognitive Bias
Renée J. Mitchell

Public Corruption in the United States
Analysis of a Destructive Phenomenon
Jeff Cortese

The Wicked Problems of Police Reform in Canada
Laura Huey, Lorna Ferguson & Jennifer L. Schulenberg

Human Rights Policing
Reimagining Law Enforcement in the 21st Century
Peter Marina & Pedro Marina

Interviewing Vulnerable Suspects
Safeguarding the Process
Edited by Dr Jane Tudor-Owen, Dr Celine van Golde, Dr Ray Bull & David Gee MBE

Human Rights Policing

Reimagining Law Enforcement in the
21st Century

Peter Marina and Pedro Marina

Routledge
Taylor & Francis Group

NEW YORK AND LONDON

Cover image: © Getty Images

First published 2023
by Routledge
605 Third Avenue, New York, NY 10158

and by Routledge
4 Park Square, Milton Park, Abingdon, Oxon, OX14 4RN

Routledge is an imprint of the Taylor & Francis Group, an informa business

© 2023 Peter Marina and Pedro Marina

Library of Congress Cataloging-in-Publication Data
Names: Marina, Peter, 1976– author. | Marina, Pedro, author.
Title: Human rights policing : reimagining law enforcement in the 21st century / Peter Marina, Pedro Marina.
Description: New York, NY : Routledge, 2023. | Series: Routledge series on practical and evidence-based policing | Includes bibliographical references and index.
Identifiers: LCCN 2022012935 (print) | LCCN 2022012936 (ebook) | ISBN 9781032115221 (hardback) | ISBN 9781032115191 (paperback) | ISBN 9781003220282 (ebook)
Subjects: LCSH: Police. | Human rights. | Police-community relations.
Classification: LCC HV7921 .M369 2023 (print) | LCC HV7921 (ebook) | DDC 363.2/3–dc23/eng/20220604
LC record available at https://lccn.loc.gov/2022012935
LC ebook record available at https://lccn.loc.gov/2022012936

ISBN: 978-1-032-11522-1 (hbk)
ISBN: 978-1-032-11519-1 (pbk)
ISBN: 978-1-003-22028-2 (ebk)

DOI: 10.4324/9781003220282

Typeset in Bembo
by Newgen Publishing UK

Dedicated to those who want to protect and serve the human rights of all people.

In memory of our family who made the courageous journeys from Spain, to Cuba, to the shores of Miami to New Orleans and New York.

Contents

Acknowledgments

For the first author, the writing of this book took place in order of the following places: New Orleans, USA; San Cristobal de las Casas (Chiapas), Mexico; New York, USA; Guadalajara, Mexico; Athens and Crete, Greece; Bucharest, Romania; Rome, Bologna, Naples, and Milan Italy; Mexico City, Oaxaca City, Cancun (Centro), Tulum, La Paz, and Tijuana Mexico; San Diego and Slab City, California. The last words of the book were written in the California desert. Few experiences surpass the joy of travel and writing. A shout to all who possess the traveler's soul.

It's not often father and son—two best friends—get to write a book together. We hope that our experiences and thoughts produced in this book will do some good in the world.

Without my mother, a woman of rare passion and total devotion, this book would be impossible. She's the strength of the family, as is often the case with women, particularly when married to a cop. Together, we all conceived of this book in Northern Spain (Galicia, Asturias, and Basque regions) during our epic adventure to rediscover our ancestors. What a dream trip that will last forever in our memories. Viva España. Viva Cuba Libre.

The university used to be a place of intellectual curiosity, an arena of thought that challenged power and orthodoxy. Sociology, right at the center of university life, used to possess a magic that rocked the world of those who employed its imagination. Sociology once asked the big questions, challenged capitalism and imperialism, confronted colonialism and oppression, questioned authority and hierarchy, and called for radical new ideas to understand the current historical epoch. Real sociologists sacrificed their careers for the pursuit of truth. It seems so much of that magic is gone today in many American universities. It breaks my heart. But I keep the sociological imagination alive in my heart and soul, and the romance of the liberal arts and humanities still exists within the very fabric of my being. I'll always expose my students to the magic and thrill of sociology; they deserve to know the great high of getting exposed to new ideas that shake the foundations of our existence.

As for me, I live in existential freedom, not just in an attitude toward life, but a pure freedom that allows my soul to parade and dance. It frightens some people. I suspect some fear true freedom, and that fear makes some people cower, project, and act out in that fear. But freedom is a rare condition that I wish to share with others. I wish they could feel the freedom that lies in the deepest part of my being. Love to all those who understand this freedom, and best wishes to those yet to find it.

Thanks to my colleagues David Gladstone, Jane Mooney, David Brotherton, the late Jock Young, the late Barry Spunt, Louis Kontos, Terry Williams, and Danny Kessler, among many others. As Danny says, "Joy against the machine; rage when necessary." You ready to get "Marinated" Kessler?

Thanks to other scholars who have influenced my thinking such as Edward Green, Jeff Farrell, Simon Hallsworth, Elijah Anderson, and Keith Hayward. Thanks to the other scholars who pursue truth no matter the consequences such as David Harvey, Noam Chomsky, Norman Finkelstein, Ward Churchill, and all the wonderful critical, radical, and mad thinkers of the world.

Thanks to my friends Jim Lightfoot, Carl Meine, Pierre Bollók, and Dora Zetina.

Thanks to my best friend Dr. G.

Thanks to those who support me at the university including Victor Macias-Gonzalez and Mike Haupert.

Thanks to Annette Valeo for all her support on human rights policing. Thanks to Allen Hill and Mike Valencia, two outstanding people. Thanks to Ron Camacho, Christopher Schuster, David Pehl, Ryan Slosser, and to the many other devoted police officers who serve their profession well. Thanks to all those who have taken our human rights policing classes.

Thanks to Paul Marina, Elena Marina, and Mike Scott. Special thanks to the four-legged creatures Abbie and Fannie and Lagniappe and their wonderful bellies. In memory of Peaches, Kelly, and Dixie. Thanks to J.J., Dr. Gonzo, Pavo, Pollo, Ms. Mirl, Clementine, Juniper, sweet Willow, Sanford, and Chaya.

To everyone in New Orleans, who dat baby. NOLA always. Yeah, you right, darlin'.

Thanks to all the great people throughout history who advanced the goals of human rights in society. Love to all the animals of the world where human rights is not even a consideration. My heart will always break for you, and one day I hope to alleviate some of your suffering. Human rights belong to all conscious, sentient beings existing in this universe.

To my true love.

Peter Marina—New Orleans, 2022

A Preface from the Second Author
Lt. Pedro Marina (Retired)

Human rights policing, what a noble expression! Can we truly achieve it? Of course, the answer is yes. But it takes education in the concept and training to implement it.

And, in spite of all the publicity about so many people dying at the hands of police in the past few years, there is hope, and police departments show willingness to institute changes. Change is what this book is all about. That is why all police professionals must read this book.

Change in police training started a long time ago and continues today. Not long ago I was talking to a police sergeant who was telling me that when he went through the police academy, he learned how to violate Fourth Amendment rights. Curiously, I asked how does that happen? He said that when patrolling an area with a reputation for drug trafficking, he would go to individuals he suspected of drug dealing and pat them down. He added that if he felt a bulge in the subject's pocket that may possibly be contraband, he would place the subject under arrest. Once a person is under arrest, any search incidental to the arrest is legal and would stand in court. He mentioned that police officers often search such people, find contraband, and arrest. A criminal court would most likely find this type of search illegal under the Fourth Amendment. This was just an effective way to get around the Fourth Amendment protection. I must say that I was not totally shocked. It was not my first time hearing of the scheme. Well, police academies don't teach that any more. In fact, teaching community policing seems now the norm.

But more must change. Another police officer from another jurisdiction recently told me that his agency prohibits any kind of pursuit. Angrily, he said that when patrolling, a vehicle may pass him exceeding the speed limit. He added that if he tries to stop the vehicle, he cannot pursue if the driver decides to ignore him. He mentioned that this tended to demoralize the department. And, I agree with the demoralizing part. The solution is to get police out of traffic enforcement. Let police do real police work. But that is not to say that if a vehicle driving recklessly poses extreme danger to the community that police should not try to stop that vehicle, not so much for a traffic offense but for the danger it poses to the community.

We can continue a dialogue on how police departments are changing to become more accountable to their communities. This is growing increasingly evident. For the past many years departments have sought not only to have more diversity in their ranks, but to give those more of a voice in the conduct of police work.

The evidence of change is apparent, but we still have a long way to go. As a retired police officer in a major metropolitan city, I still love the profession and want to share what I have learned in the many years and many assignments going up through ranks. So, when the opportunity came along with my son Peter, a criminologist, to put our knowledge and experience to work, we teamed up and created this book centering around human rights. We hope that the reader gets to understand all the material we present in this book—all leading to a new vision for law enforcement in the 21st century that focuses on human rights policing.

Introduction

Interested in finding new ways to improve the institution of law enforcement? Want to become even better police officers? Want to foster improved trust between law enforcement agents and the communities they protect and serve? Is it time to end notions of an "us" against "them" mentality? Is it time the police and community built better rapport?

Tired of self-proclaimed "social justice warriors" beating over your head *their* concept of white privilege and toxic patriarchy while advancing *their* careers? Frustrated with a world seemingly turning against cops and blaming them for rising crime rates? Finding a sense of disquiet at people accusing you of racism? Feeling personally attacked from outsiders who think all cops are rotten? Weary of culturally appropriated "wokism" ideology asking you to denounce yourself for the level of melanin in your skin? Tired of uncritical "critical" lectures preaching righteousness from ivory towers? Ever been accused of being an "Uncle Tom" or selling out your own black and brown brothers and sisters? Ever been called a "bitch" for doing police work? Ever had colleagues ostracize you for remaining true to your principles? Question "professionals" judging you for doing a job they know little about? Skeptical of academics constantly blaming you for white supremacy, or upholding white supremacy? Equally skeptical of councilors, journalists, and professional development careerists telling you what to think instead of how to think? Ever want to challenge those who want to force their ideology and dogmatic beliefs on you?

Do you possess intellectual curiosity? Do you fancy yourself capable of independent thought? Do you think beyond the proverbial box? Do you want to think in new and creative ways? Do you want to further understand your profession? Do you believe law enforcement agents can make a more positive difference in society? Do you question political orthodoxy? Do you want to challenge yourself?

Do you have big questions about the world today? Do you question the criminal justice system? Do you wonder about your role in society? Are you willing to engage in self-reflection and critique? Do you want to improve as a human, and further, as a law enforcement professional? Do you wonder how you can make a difference? Do you want to transcend the ordinary?

If you stated yes to any of the above questions, this book is for you.

This ain't your daddy's rodeo.

This book will not tell you what to think or believe. Instead, this book will give you intellectual tools on how to think. We want to help bring out your full creative potential as law enforcement agents, police officers, and criminal justice system professionals and advocates.

It starts with human rights and how to apply it to police work.

Here's a taste. It's the New Orleans Police Department and the city of sin and debauchery.

DOI: 10.4324/9781003220282-1

Suicide-by-Cop: A Code Two Call in the New Orleans Police Department

I'm a lieutenant, platoon commander for the second watch working 2:25 pm to 11 pm, with almost 30 years serving the New Orleans Police Department and the great people of the Big Easy. I've seen too much death, and fear another death is imminent.

The call was a priority of a Code 2, requiring lights and sirens. As I hit the pedal to the metal, I began to reflect on my policing career.

Police work is unique in many aspects. There are times of boredom and times of extreme excitement. The job goes on for 24 hours, seven days a week. One does not stop being the police simply because one is off-duty. And then, there's the power and responsibility that comes with it. In my nearly 30 years of police work, I found that it is the power and not the so obvious responsibility that comes with that power that plays a major part in the life of a police officer. The power of police comes with every aspect of the job. Certainly, the ability to take anyone's freedom and the use of force, sometimes deadly force is foremost in the mind of police officers.

Today's a typical day in my district. When we hit the street, as usual, there was a backlog of calls for service. However, by late afternoon we managed to clear the backlog. Then the call came. A signal 107, a suspicious character, a black man wearing a blue shirt and blue jeans sitting on a bench along the riverfront with one hand under a newspaper. A concerned citizen passing by called it in. The call was a priority of a Code 2, requiring lights and sirens.

The first officer arriving on the scene informed the dispatcher that he had spotted the subject in question sitting on a bench. The officer said that he tried to approach the subject asking him to take his hand from under the newspaper and show both hands. He added that when the subject refused to comply, he backed away and took cover behind the police car while still maintaining a visual on the subject. As I proceeded to the scene, I instructed other cars responding to set up a perimeter a safe distance from the subject. By the time I arrived, there were five police cars side-to-side about 40 feet from the bench where the man was still sitting. I parked my vehicle along that perimeter and immediately spotted the man fitting the dispatcher's description broadcast. I exited the car and called out to the man to show both hands and explained that we just wanted to talk to him. The man showed no response. He sat motionless. I instructed all my officers to maintain their positions until we got some reaction from the man. Then, several minutes passed by as I continued to talk to the man assuring him that he had broken no law and we just wanted to talk to him to be sure that he was safe.

A few more minutes passed when the man got up and started walking toward my police car with his hand still under the newspaper. My car was the last in a semicircle around him. As he approached the police cars, I kept pleading with him to stop and show his hands. Then the unexpected happened. The two officers whose vehicle was at the end of the perimeter managed to go some distance around the man totally unseen. I could see that the man was getting closer to the police cars in a very threatening manner with his hand still under the newspaper. As the time was getting shorter and shorter for a decision, the two officers continued their slow approach still unseen and unheard. At approximately ten feet behind, the officer made their move, running toward the man and tackling him to the ground. They held both of his arms, exposing a .38 caliber revolver. It was apparent. This incident was going to be a suicide either by police or self-inflicted. As the officer lifted the man and handcuffed him a small crowd had gathered behind the police cars. They began to applaud the actions of those two brave police officers. It was well deserved. I should point out that the subject was transported to mental facility and no charges were filed.

Later that evening as I was dismissing the platoon, I talked to those two police officers to express my gratitude. I asked them to explain what they had done. The officers told me that far too often in their careers they had seen similar situations of suicide by police. They said there had to be another way to end these situations. But then I interrupted saying that they put themselves at risk. With a smile on their faces, they replied: "No, lieutenant we have guns and we know how to use them, we felt that the odds were in our favor, saving the life of one man was worth the small risk." It was obvious to me that these two officers had respect for the human rights of the people in their community.

Years later, while discussing the potential of human rights policing with my son, I became aware of that awesome power of the concept of human rights, and further, that it has to be ever present in the daily activities of police officers. Without the personal recognition of human rights, police officers can appear to be uncaring at best and bullies at worst. I propose that a "good" police officer keeps the concept of human rights ever present in every action that he or she takes. Without it, he or she may or may not survive to retirement. Further, without the concept of human rights "front and center" in one's heart and mind, an officer lacks the perspective that he or she is dealing with human beings, not "characters," criminals, or suspects. When the officer lacks that human rights awareness, there can be deadly consequences.

The situation above, I later realized, illustrates how human rights saved the life of a human being. I now know that how the concept of human rights policing plays a major role in saving lives. How many lives will you save too?

Welcome to human rights policing.

Chapter 1

Human Rights Policing

Introduction

This intense scene of a real-life "suicide-by-cop" situation, taken from first-hand experience of the second author in the line of duty, highlights the central theme of this book—applying human rights to police work. Human rights move beyond an officer's legal obligation to uphold civil rights, rather, it involves reaching higher standards of policing in a world that needs, now perhaps more than ever, the best police work that law enforcement has to offer. If human rights became the focus of the world's global economic, political, environmental, and military policies, perhaps the world would look much healthier, even further, perhaps we could solve our most pressing social problems. But applying human rights starts at an individual and community level. This book asks members of law enforcement and criminal justice professionals and advocates to take the first courageous steps toward making human rights a reality.[1] We believe that you can become the harbingers of change in a world that desperately needs it. Up to the challenge? Care to make a difference?

This chapter introduces readers to human rights policing, argues for human rights in extraordinary times, discusses the goals of human rights policing, shares the second author's reflections on 30 years of policing, and offers important points of departure for the book. At the end of the chapter, we ask readers how they define human rights, how important are human rights to policing today, and if they have ever thought about applying human rights to their everyday police work.

Human Rights in Extraordinary Times

Human civilization uneasily sits in a precarious moment in history. To a growing segment of the population, the current structural arrangement of society seems highly peculiar—a system rigged for those who possess tremendous wealth and power. Our late modern world is a time of rapid social transformation and extraordinary change. It's a time of uncertainty and doubt, fear and risk, ontological insecurity and existential threat, and the growing instability in our personal lives involving family, work, community, and interpersonal relationships. Social transformation and societal change create the conditions of anomie where people increasingly feel disconnected from their communities and institutions. The contradictions of everyday life and the constant blurring of realities in this reified social world only intensify the precariousness of these uncertain times. The sturdy ground on which we once confidently walked now seems dangerously shaky.

Marx best characterizes the experience of the modern world as a time where "all that is solid melts in air, all that is holy is profaned, and man is at last compelled with sober senses to face his real conditions of life." As all the certainty of the world seems to melt into thin air, and

DOI: 10.4324/9781003220282-2

as the recognizable world disappears into an unknown, hostile facticity hovering somewhere above, the tendency is to close our eyes and hold on even tighter to a world slipping away. But still some people desperately hold on while wondering about the conditions shaping their life.

In the era some scholars describe as liquid modernity, people look for ways to ameliorate the conditions causing discomfort, unease, and discontent. But many people today grow increasingly aware that they have somehow lost control over the events and circumstances shaping their lives. What's more, people find themselves awakening to the reality that their political and economic elites abandoned them. It seems that those commanding the centers of power, including the major political parties of the Western world, sold the people out long ago for their own self-interests, or for the interests of their corporate masters, or as Adam Smith calls them "The Masters of Mankind." Politicians on the left and right sides of the political spectrum appeal to the masses with nice teleprompter words from writers skilled in the power of persuasion, mass manipulation, and propaganda. But the fantastic words spewed rarely find realization—words without substance, bark without bite. People increasingly feel impotent to shape the world beyond the immediate private orbit of their own lives, and now even control of their personal lives slips away. The symptoms of such a world manifest themselves in our everyday lives.

We live in a time of increased poverty and homelessness, social disruption and crime, suicide and depression, addiction and joblessness, mass shootings and acts of brutality, needless violence and domestic abuse, forever wars and invasions, inflation and rising economic costs, and the growing instability of work, community, family, and interpersonal relationships impacting billions of people around the globe. Our political and economic elite give us ready-made stories of all the culprits behind this suffering.

The politicians on the right blame the liberals, socialists and communists, Black Lives Matter activists, ANTIFA, Muslims, undocumented immigrants (the mis-named) social justice warriors, wokists, democrats, China, Reagan's welfare queens, Clinton's super-predators, inner-city kids, street gangs, culture wars and identity politics, and declining family values that rip us apart.

On the flip side of the proverbial coin, the politicians on the so-called left create their own folk devils to blame for the social ills of the day.[2] They blame the current state of discontent on republicans, cops and law enforcement agents, conservatives, far right-wing groups, white nationalists and racists, gun-toting rioters, Russian spies, and anyone who does not faithfully and dutifully agree with the liberal orthodoxy of identity politics, white privilege, and toxic patriarchy.

The political and economic elite, along with the corporate media serving their interests, create these categories that artificially divide us against one another. These categories serve as weapons of propaganda used to manufacture consent to the status quo.

What's interesting is that those who command the centers of power never blame themselves or the political and economic systems they control. While they control the material conditions that shape our lives, they refuse to accept responsibility for the huge toll of human suffering created under these conditions. Instead, they manufacture political ideologies using "us against them" tactics that divide us on matters such as nationality and religion, race and ethnicity, sex and gender, cop and gang member, criminal and law-abiding citizen, documented or illegal, patriotic or un-American, liberal or conservative, and so on. They even shape the framework for oppositional discourse that does not allow resistance from views that go against the socially accepted status quo. What they don't tell us is that we sit politically and economically closer to each other than to the people we elect to, supposedly, solve our problems and represent our interests. It's the proverbial divide-and-conquer strategy, and it's largely working. Destroy the solidarity of the people (dare we say class solidarity?) and the people will never know the true causes of the social problems plaguing a world increasingly up for grabs. While we battle each other on the streets, the rich and powerful who command our society grow their wealth and power exponentially, even during the greatest pandemic of the 21st century.[3] Why do we allow this to happen? What can we do about this?

The political and economic elite, on both the right and left, will not solve the social problems of the day. In fact, they exacerbate the challenges humanity faces both as a collective species and as individuals confronting social problems on a daily basis. Simply voting for a better world will not suffice. There is no charismatic figure coming to save the people. There is no political party that will ease the concerns and ameliorate the troubles of the world. Instead, it's up the people to make the changes necessary for a better society. We bear the responsibility to take action for the creation of a better world. The key to making social change relies on finding a sense of solidarity with people from all walks of life, regardless of our differences.

We can resist the propaganda and categories imposed on us.

There is another way forward.

People can learn to think for themselves and find common grounds on the issues that unite us together across the political spectrum. People can work together to advance their common interests for a better society. We believe that if human rights policing is possible, it proves that all people can work together for a future that belongs to all of us.

Late modern society is a time of radical change and heightened social transformation that hastens feelings of precariousness and uncertainty. But these feelings of fear and risk also bring about an extraordinary opportunity for creativity and imagination where we can discover ourselves in new and highly exciting ways.

The spectrum of change is upon us. The decision of where to move this moving juggernaut remains yet to be made. This current historical moment offers the possibility to explore new avenues of thought and freedom, modes of intellect and expression, abilities to reach self-actualization and self-transcendence, chances for exploration and adventure, and ways to reinvent the self and transcend the ordinary. We have an increasing capacity to resist norms and orthodoxy, go beyond our prescribed social roles and scripts, and to constantly rewrite our narratives and make new stories that define our lives. Whether old or young, urban or rural, married or single, conservative or liberal, we have the opportunity to change, evolve, and become something new. We can respond in new ways to our social world, create new paths forward, develop new ways of understanding and reflection, plow new paths for action, and make a world in our own image that reflects our heart and soul. In short, we can become more. You can become more.

Interested?

People have more in common than they realize. I, the first author, have traveled extensively in both the Western and Eastern world and to remote regions far beyond to find, among other things, that people share the same essential qualities. We love our families and friends, get our hearts devastatingly broken, and break hearts ourselves. We cheer our sports teams and run to save the life of a stranger in peril. We dance in the streets, sing in existential celebration, and hold the one we love ever so close. We hide our greatest fears and keep secret our deepest insecurities while feigning a confident smile and mask of joy. We all hold strong to hopes of the future and imagine ourselves as stars making change. We get disappointed and find that, in turn, we disappoint our dearest friends and family. We fail all the time but somehow stand again. We search for meaning and believe that in the end all will be fine; somehow, we won't end in that eternal goodnight. We surprise even ourselves with extreme acts of altruism and selflessness, only to realize our acts of greed a short time later. We tell jokes simply to make strangers smile while angrily shout at others for the smallest of inconveniences. We fancy our-selves fair only to find our extreme acts of judgment and prejudice, and wonder how to get better.

We want love, safety, comfort, beauty, protection, security, dignity, and to witness all the bursting colors of life that fulfill our imaginations and expand our hearts and minds. We want to love more and be loved, reach new depths of consciousness while also wanting the simple pleasures of life: the sounds of church bells in the distance, the peal of a kid's laughter, the little smile on your loved one's face, the look of an adoring son or daughter, the joy of leaving work headed for a two-day break, the excitement of a Saturday night when everything's clicking just right, the familiar notes of a favorite song from one's more youthful days, the hug from the son or daughter after months away, the first sip of beer after a day's work, a glass of wine with fine tunes in the background, the hurt of disappointing your son or daughter, the joy of redemption and forgiveness, the cat purring on your lap, the precious times spent with loved ones when you know time increasingly slips away, the dog so happy to see you like it's been 12 months and one day, the overwhelming emotions you get when helping someone in need, the smell of your parent's cologne or perfume, the taste of coffee in the morning, the pitter-patter thumping of the heart when one falls hopelessly in love, and the moment you first land in a new country and get your mind blown. We are different, yes, but in so many ways we are the same, hiding ourselves within the shell of these time-limited bodies. We want to be alive for the first time, transcend our immediate experience, find meaning in a world, and connect to others in love and solidarity and belonging. Our hearts beat for the same reasons.

In short, humans share many of the same interests, concerns, hopes, and dreams. If they realize their common interests, perhaps they can make meaningful change in this world and ease some of its suffering. Perhaps people on all sides of the political spectrum—from the far right to the far left and everywhere in between—can find common ground to work together to advance a common cause. Perhaps, together, we can find a way to not only survive but prosper. This takes people putting aside some of their differences to achieve a higher goal.

A tall task indeed, but it takes small steps to start the process. This book invites you to take that small step.

This book asks you to analyze the meaning of human rights and what it means for not only your careers as law enforcement and criminal justice professionals and advocates, but also for your personal lives. Change and uncertainty offer extraordinary possibilities for you and the world you inhabit. It starts with human rights, and it applies to your careers that help keep the world safe, and, potentially, make it better.

Goals of the Book: What Do We Want? Human Rights! Who's Gonna Protect it? Cops!

If the title above fails to provide a subtle indication about the book's goals, how about "Who dat say dey gonna apply human rights to policing?" Cops dat! Cops dat! In the Big Easy we often chant "who dat" in the Superdome rooting on the N.F.L. professional franchise the New Orleans Saints. But our change in phrase captures the goals of the book—to apply human rights to everyday policing. Applying human rights goes beyond virtue signaling, or occasion-ally applying human rights when convenient, or consistently applying one version or perspec-tive of human rights. Rather, applying human rights requires extensive, intended, purposive, hyper-conscious, and highly active thought and action toward one's everyday police work. It requires thinking of new and creative ways to apply human rights to a variety of specific situ-ations. It takes a life-long process of examination, analysis, self-reflection, and self-critique of one's thoughts and actions while on the job and beyond.

We, as authors, make no attempt to tell you what thoughts, feelings, or values you should possess on party affiliation, race and ethnicity, mass incarceration, the war on drugs, immigration, religion, identity politics, sex and gender, or any other matter. We can't know what's in your heart, and it's none of our business. This book refuses to engage in any type of thought correction often found in places like China's cultural revolution, and to a certain degree, in many American universities today. Human rights policing is not about becoming more aware of micro-aggressions, white supremacy in Western society, understanding white privilege, or becoming an "anti-racist." Rather, regardless of your personal thoughts, views, and feelings, our goal is to help you apply human rights to your everyday police interactions with members of the community. We will challenge you to think in new and creative ways about the meaning of human rights and how it can be applied to every situation you encounter as police officers and law enforcement professionals.

In short, this book provides law enforcement agents a guide on how to apply human rights to their law enforcement careers. The book uses data collected from years of interviewing and observing police officers as well as on information gathered from police officer's experiences. The book explores how we, and others in law enforcement, understand and interpret human rights as well as how law enforcement professionals apply it to their careers. Police officers who have conducted interviews with diverse members of their community will discuss what community members want police officers to know about human rights and serving their community.

While we discuss throughout the book issues related to the criminal justice system, mass incarceration, the war on drugs, and the structural causes of crime, we always bring it back front-and-center to a police-officer-informed application of human rights policing. Each chapter develops the reader's ability to deeply consider human rights and how they may be applied to various policing scenarios. Toward the end of the book, we provide rich and layered content from police officers who have contributed their personal stories on how they applied human rights policing to real-world events encountered in their jobs. The task is left up to you to develop creative ways to implement human rights policing to a wide variety of situations you experience in your everyday police work.

Who Are We?

The first author is a professor, the second a retired police officer. Together we created a human rights policing certificate program that instructs police officers and criminal justice professionals on how to apply human rights to their jobs. We use data based on observation and research with police officers collected over the course of many years. We became acquainted with the unique perspectives of current and retired police officers who have discussed with us the meaning of human rights and how they apply it to police work. In this way, we take a more egalitarian approach using the contributions of law enforcement agents to help guide the reader on how to apply human rights policing to their everyday jobs. Our experiences, combined with the experiences of diverse police officers who have contributed to this book, provide rich content and authentic perspectives that, we believe, equip us well to successfully write a book teaching police officers how to apply human rights to their professional careers.

The first author is a sociologist and criminologist who uses immersive ethnographic research to delve into previously unfamiliar worlds and cultures to make sense of human realities. In this book, we rely on extensive ethnographic research observing and interviewing police officers from around the United States while also conducting dozens of police ride-alongs. In those years of research as a trained sociologist (and cop's son), I, the first author, learned much about how police officers think and what makes them tick. Of course, it helps that "police blood" runs in the family, but it also helps to have the trained professional eye of the sociologist to observe police behavior, listen to them talk about their lives, values, beliefs, and motivations. I've also built personal relationships with police officers who continue to share their ideas with me, and help inform my thoughts and ideas on how to develop a book to help law enforcement agents apply human rights to policing.

This book also relies on the experience of a former New Orleans police officer. The second author (father of the first author) is a retired New Orleans Police Lieutenant for the New Orleans Police Department with 30 years of law enforcement experience in the Big Easy. He graduated from the University of New Orleans with a degree in sociology and joined the New Orleans Police Department in 1975. Before being promoted to the Civil Service rank of sergeant he served in the Vice Crime Section, the Second Police District in uptown New Orleans as a patrol officer, the Robbery Unit of the Major Crimes Division, The Special Operations Bureau as a SWAT officer and 12 years as a narcotics agent. After being promoted to sergeant, he served in the Eighth District in the New Orleans French Quarter as a platoon supervisor before returning to the Narcotics Section as a platoon commander. While serving in that section, Sergeant Marina was promoted to the rank of lieutenant and reassigned to the Eighth District as platoon commander. Lieutenant Marina retired from the Third Police District where he was serving as a platoon commander. During his career the Lieutenant received numerous awards for exemplary performance in the line of duty. This priceless wealth of knowledge is layered throughout the text.

Aside from our experiences, our consultation with police officers contributed to the content and relevance of this book. In addition to their personal experiences of the job, these professionals shared their understanding of human rights, including their interpretations of the United Nation's Declaration of Human Rights. The police officers we have consulted contributed to this book, applying their wealth of knowledge and experiences to share with the reader their understanding of human rights and how they apply it to their jobs.

Reflections on 30 Years of Policing: Thoughts for the Reader

Police work, police officer as a profession, what an adventure! I, the second author, can't think of a more exciting and rewarding career. And that excitement is still there today for young women and men coming into the profession. It certainly was there when I came on in the summer of 1975. But what makes this job so exciting as a career? What does it take to keep that enthusiasm all the way to retirement?

I propose to you that the secret to a long career is adaptation to the ever-present changes in the profession guided by your moral compass. Of course, that compass has be nurtured in your mind constantly. Here is my revelation: this course on human rights for police officers will go a long way toward the nurturing of that moral compass so necessary for public service, especially law enforcement. A simple definition of human rights can be found in a Google search. "Human rights are the basic rights and freedoms that belong to every person in the world, from birth until death." These basic rights are based on shared values like dignity, fairness, equality, respect, and independence. These values are defined and protected by the United Nations Declaration of Human Rights. Your moral compass must embrace this concept of human rights in every action that you take and every word that you utter.

But police departments are not all that good at shaping an individual's moral compass in their training from the recruitment academy to ongoing professional training. Sure, they have hundreds of rules and policies governing behavior, from the use of deadly force to the issuing of a traffic citation. But the moral compass assistance is not there. But it needs to be there.

For far too long police academies teach young women and men, for the most part, in their early twenties, about state law, municipal ordinances, traffic laws, supreme court decisions, department regulations, and so forth. Lacking in that training is the moral aspect of that enforcement. And make no mistake, every encounter a police officer has needs to be in the context of their moral compass guiding them to recognize and act from awareness of human rights. Legal action does not equal action with respect for human rights actions.

That last statement is illustrated by a conversation I had with a young narcotics officer. He described to me that part of his job was to stop narcotics trafficking especially in the many street corners of the city where dope was openly sold. When he told me that, I immediately exclaimed that I assumed that what he did was legal. He responded that, of course, his actions were legal.

Then I said yes, I know there are many street corners where there is a constant traffic of illicit drugs. The one that comes to my mind is Gallier and Law Streets in the city of New Orleans. Oh, he said, he was very familiar with that corner. He explained that he and his partner would often target that intersection. He said that there was usually a group of men at the intersection. Some were homeless people, some drunks, some people just "hanging out" there, some just passing by, and some, in fact, dealing dope just waiting for customers to arrive and make a purchase. I said, well, how do you know the difference when you approach the corner. I usually don't know who is doing what, he responded, so I ask everybody to put their hands on the wall for a pat down. I base this action on the reputation of the corner for drug dealing, my own experience in observing drug transactions there, and the fact that drug dealers often carry weapons. So, for my own safety I pat them down for weapons. Then he added that there were times when during that pat down he would discover what could be an illicit drug such as crack cocaine. He added that he would then place the subject under arrest, and search incidental to arrest. The whole thing was legal, he insisted.

Sometime after I spoke to this police officer, I began to run this whole scenario through my head with an emphasis, not on the legality of the officer's action, but on the aspect of respect for human rights. The officer said that there were many people just standing on those street corners not selling or buying drugs, as well as people just passing by on their way to a particular destination. While it is legally questionable whether he can approach them or pat them down, I leave that decision on legality to the district attorney's office or a judge in court of law. However, there is no question that the unalienable "rights to dignity, fairness, equality, respect and independence" of at least some of those people on that particular corner, at that particular time, were violated.

I propose to you, fellow police officers, that the respect called for in the Declaration of Human Rights must be present in every action you take. I am not saying that you cannot go to those corners infested with drug dealers and make an arrest. But when you do you must make sure that you don't violate the human rights not only of those engaged in drug trafficking but also the rights of those engaged in the illicit traffic. You cannot arbitrarily stop people on a street corner who may just be passing by and are totally innocent. I am not talking about the legality. I am talking about the violation of their basic human rights to freedom, dignity, equality, and more. As a police officer you must make sure that you not only respect their legal rights, but that you enforce those legal rights. Furthermore, you must also respect their human rights as those rights are not for you to take away because those people are endowed with those rights the moment they are born.

Now, here is what appears to be a contradiction in police work, especially illustrated by the scenario presented by the narcotics officer in my conversation. That police officer actually makes arrests in what may well be a perfectly legal detention. So, how is taking someone's freedom in an arrest not a violation of human rights so explicitly mentioned in the Declaration? Implicit in that Declaration is that a society must create just and fair laws for the protection of its citizen and that call for sanctions against those who violate them. As police officers we have the power and responsibility to enforce those laws and, at times, make an arrest, that deprives someone of his or her freedom. But, take notice, we make an arrest as long as we respect the individual's rights of dignity, fairness, respect, compassion, equality, among other rights.

You will find that this book shows you the way to apply human rights policing. I joined my son, Dr. Peter Marina, the sociologist and criminologist, in creating this work to assist my fellow police officers in making a better world in which our profession not only thrives and is respected but also remains rewarding. Our profession can make even more of a positive difference in making our communities better. Join us!

Points of Departure

Civil Rights Versus Human Rights

We will assume police officers know their legal obligation to respect the civil rights of all people. This book moves beyond civil rights and into the world of human rights. Human rights involve a natural, inherent quality belonging to all members of the human species.[4] The United Nations defines human rights the following way:

> Human rights are rights inherent to all human beings, regardless of race, sex, nationality, ethnicity, language, religion, or any other status. Human rights include the right to life and liberty, freedom from slavery and torture, freedom of opinion and expression, the right to work and education, and many more. Everyone is entitled to these rights, without discrimination.
>
> (United Nations 1948)

Human rights naturally and inherently belong to all human beings regardless of their actions or thoughts. Human beings permanently possess their human rights under all conditions and at all times. Put differently, it is impossible for human beings to lose or forfeit their human rights. Furthermore, it is impossible for anyone to take away another person's human rights. People, police officers for example, can only take away, or deprive, human beings from *enjoying* the human rights that naturally and permanently belong to them. But again, it is impossible for anyone to take away the human rights of any other person.

Civil rights, on the other hand, are legal creations. Governments grant civil rights under laws of citizenship. Government constitutions, like the U.S. Constitution and its Bill of Rights, intend to protect civil rights. Civil rights serve as a social contract between citizens and their government, that is, the individual voluntarily forfeits some civil rights in exchange for certain protections. One's access to civil rights depends on citizenship of a nation-state and, unlike the permanency of universal human rights, shifts with one's change of affiliation from one government entity to another. Unlike human rights, civil rights can be taken away from human beings for all kinds of reasons, and that happens all the time.

Human rights are not legal fictions or something "granted" to the individual. People are born with human rights, meaning rights inherent at the moment of birth. No government agency, organization, institution, group, or individual can legitimately grant or deny human rights. While human rights often include the rights to life, pursuit of happiness and meaning, health care, shelter, food, dignity, education, and expression, among many others, the United Nations General Assembly adopted the widely accepted Universal Declaration of Human Rights in 1948. Human rights are universal; all humans have it at all times and all places regardless of war situations, legal status, nationality, income, or any other historical conditions or states of being.

This book focuses on human rights to show how law enforcement can reach an even higher standard of policing for the 21st century. Chapter 2 involves a deeper discussion on human rights and its application to policing.

Whose Side are We On?

We consider ourselves public servants in service to the global and local community. While we all possess different lenses through which we view reality—biases and prejudices—we are on the side of those who want to protect and serve the human rights of all people.

Regardless of your political views, sexual orientation, or your perspectives on race, class, gender, and ethnicity, if you're in the business of protecting the enjoyment of human rights for all people, we share the same goal.

Implicit Bias

Despite the claims of many social scientists and journalists, complete objectivity and value neutrality is impossible. As trained sociologists, rather than pretending to give completely "objective" and "unbiased" interpretations of social phenomenon, we admit our biases to the reader and openly navigate through them, sometimes unevenly, during the writing process. We encourage the reader to do the same, admit one's biases and prejudices about the world, reflect on them, and inquire about their origin and validity. It's best to pay full attention to one's biases and examine them rather than pretending not to have them at all. We, as authors, don't ask you to do what we are not willing to do ourselves.

We all hold biased views. This is also true for academics, especially in the liberal arts. One could argue that all of the social sciences are ideological. Many professors in the liberal arts hold orthodox and dogmatic liberal views that, to some observers, foster an anti-intellectual climate that refuses to allow challenging real structures of power. The following quote from the critical journalist Glenn Greenwald captures the essence of what's happened to journalism, and could easily be applied to academia:

> But this is now the prevailing ethos in corporate journalism. They have insufficient talent or skill, and even less desire, to take on real power centers: the military-industrial complex, the CIA and FBI, the clandestine security state, Wall Street, Silicon Valley monopolies, the corrupted and lying corporate media outlets they serve. So settling on this penny-ante, trivial bullshit—tattling, hall monitoring, speech policing: all in the most anti-intellectual, adolescent and primitive ways—is all they have. It's all they are. It's why they have fully earned the contempt and distrust in which the public holds them.
>
> (Greenwald 2021)

Some police officers, perhaps for good reason, distrust outsiders. They may take particular offense at the hubris of academics who write about cops (and gang members for that matter) they know nothing about, and often may never have even met. Professors, just like cops, hail from a wide variety of experiences and backgrounds. Academics are not all the same.

While we're critical of mainstream media, politics, journalists, and academics on both the right and left of the political spectrum, we also hold critical views on matters such as the prison industrial complex, mass incarceration, war on drugs, forever wars, environmental policies, economic inequality, and other such social problems facing human civilization. In the end, it's all about putting aside relatively minor differences compared to the monumental and, in our view, the most important task of placing in the forefront policies and ideas that advance the enjoyment of human rights for all people. We believe advancing human rights starts with policing.

Conflating the Individual and the Institution

In parts of the book, we analyze the role of various institutions, for example the criminal justice system and the prison industrial complex, in society. While we might critique these institutions, that should not necessarily be considered an indictment or attack on the people who work in those institutions.

Put differently, it's important to avoid conflating the individual and the institution. The belief goes that if an institution is evil, or severely flawed, the individual who belongs to that institution is equally evil or flawed. For example, one might think that the atomic bomb is evil, but that does not mean that those who produced atomic bombs and nuclear weapons are necessarily evil. For another example, the Nazi party was evil, but that does not mean that every Nazi soldier was equally evil. In other words, it's important to refrain from linking the institution to the individual.

Whatever flaws that might exist in the institution of law enforcement do not equate to your flaws. And, no doubt, the university today is subject, and perhaps deservedly, to critique, but this does not necessarily reflect the personal qualities of every professor. In the same way, the critiques of the institution of law enforcement are not critiques of you as an individual police officer.

We Are Verbs

We have no desire to change your thoughts, beliefs, or feelings about the world or the people in it. We simply want you to think critically about human rights and how you will apply them to policing. People tend to think of themselves, that is their identities, as constant, static entities, much like a noun. Instead, we believe that we are verbs: highly dynamic, always moving, rapidly transforming, and ever-changing over time as we move from birth to death. Perhaps we can embrace ourselves as verbs, constantly reflecting, learning new things, forging new identities, and reinventing ourselves. As Alan Watts puts it, "The more a thing tends to be permanent, the more it tends to be lifeless." Perhaps us too. Embrace change, or as Watts warns, accept existential death. We invite you to be alive, embrace change, celebrate transformation, and become more. We're all verbs in the process of becoming our best potential selves.

What Happens Next

Each chapter of the book offers a small piece of the puzzle on how to apply human rights to police work. The chapters build on each other, starting with simple concepts that become more advanced, step-by-step, with each proceeding chapter. Each chapter develops ideas explored in the previous chapter that build on each other, offering all the steps, or components, necessary to advance the goals of human rights policing. As a result, each chapter should be read in the designed order to see how each idea advances to the next in each chapter, culminating in a clear path on how to both understand and apply human rights policing to the work of law enforcement and criminal justice professionals. Each chapter ends with suggested activities, practice exercises, and thinking tips related to the main theme of the chapter with the goal of creating new ideas on how to advance human rights policing.

Chapter 2: Connecting Human Rights to Policing calls on police officers to unite under the concept of human rights policing while discussing the meaning and evolution of human rights, the United Nations Declaration of Human Rights, and the International Covenant on Civil and Political Rights, and finally a discussion of human rights from the perspective of various police officers. We develop a three-fold typology—on what we call "Human Rights Policing Social Interactions"—to explain how police officers can apply human rights in their interactions with community members. We offer examples of each type of policing social interact ion using stories from the N.O.P.D. In the end, Chapter 2 asks readers to apply what they learn in the chapter to give examples of the three types of police social interactions and to discuss three human rights they find most important to policing, their interpretation of those rights, and why they find them most important to policing.

Chapter 3: Police, Power, Agency, and Human Rights questions who watches the watchman. The chapter discusses the definition and meaning of power, where power derives, and the great philosophical debate between human agency and determinism. The chapter continues with an in-depth discussion on the meaning and potential for human agency, and more importantly, the possibilities for applying human agency to human rights policing. The chapter also offers a discussion on threats to the application of human rights looking at moral panics and the manufacturing of folk devils, while providing an example from the British television show *Black Mirror*. The chapter asks the reader, "What do you see? … How will you, as a police officer, treat the individual: as a folk devil, or as a human being deserving of their rights?" In the end, we ask readers to apply what they learn from the chapter to discuss if they believe in the potential for human agency, how they apply their human agency to police work, the importance for human agency to achieve the goals of human rights policing, and how to police those deemed folk devils.

Chapter 4: The Sociological Imagination and Human Rights Policing introduces the sociological imagination as a tool for understanding people and the world they inhabit. We offer a brief discussion on the meaning of the sociological imagination and how to use it when looking at people and their community. Since we, as authors, serve the discipline of criminology, we offer examples from criminology to discuss how to use the sociological imagination to understand the world beyond the subjective experiences of our own lives. The chapter strives to impart the sociological imagination upon readers so they can use it to better understand their communities, and, further, better protect and serve them while conducting police work. We continue with a discussion on the relationship between storytelling and human rights. People have the right to tell their own stories, but oftentimes, academics, journalists, and various media platforms strip people of their voice and right to self-representation, leading to violations of human rights and dignity. In the end, we ask the reader to apply the lessons learned in this chapter on the sociological imagination to a member of the community in which you experienced a negative interaction, or to someone you have arrested, to tell the story of the "other" from the perspective of the community member to capture the actor's point of view.

Chapter 5: Engaging with the Community on Human Rights starts with—what we call "soulful policing"—or the ability of police officers to engage in a form of policing that takes into account how members of the community make sense of, and give meaning to, their own experiences. Soulful policing is the search for "it"—or the ability to become aware and find out more about the communities law enforcement agents police. It requires police officers to develop a new, creative, and unique "police imagination" to figure out the "it" about the communities they protect and serve for the advancement of human rights policing. Learning about the community involves getting the seat of your pants dirty—Chicago School sociology style—and going into the community where social life takes place. It requires going into the bodegas, corner stories, bars, boxing gyms, churches, schools, community events, retail stores, restaurants, and small businesses of the communities police officers protect and serve to understand the world from the perspectives of community members. In short, we invite police officers to put on their sociological lens to become a Chicago School style ethnographic researcher to learn about social life in their community to advance the goals of human rights policing.

Chapter 6: Policy Suggestions, Human Rights, and the Future of Policing provides a brief summary of how each chapter served as a process leading up to an understanding of human rights and how to apply it to policing. We discuss the differences between applying kindness and human rights to our interactions with community members while performing police work. We also talk about the "blasé attitude" as a threat to human rights policing and call on law enforcement officers to resist the temptation of developing such at attitude. In the end, we make important general policy recommendation at national level as well as policy recommendations for policing as we reimagine law enforcement in the 21st century. Our conclusion offers some final thoughts on the future of policing and human rights as we push toward the later stages of modernity.

Suggested Audios, Videos, and Activities

Activity One

Please respond to the various questions:

(1) How would you define human rights? How important is it for policing today?
(2) Have you ever thought about applying human rights to your everyday police work? Either way, explain.
(3) Do you believe police officers can be powerful agents for change in society? Do you think human rights fits in this equation? Explain.
(4) The second author provided some reflection on his experiences as a police officer. Have you found time for reflection in your policing career? If so, what are some of these reflections? What advice would you offer to those newer to the field than you?
(5) Are you intrigued about the possibilities and potential of human rights policing? Explain.

Audio

Watch the following short NPR audios and videos on the history of policing in the United States. While we don't have to agree with their point of view, the videos offer insight into how some people understand the history of policing. While many would argue policing is different today, some scholars argue that we must understand the past to make sense of the present, especially if we want to push toward a better future.

> www.npr.org/2020/06/13/876628302/the-history-of-policing-and-race-in-the-u-s-are-deeply-intertwined
> www.npr.org/2020/06/05/871083599/the-history-of-police-in-creating-social-order-in-the-u-s
> www.npr.org/2020/06/05/870227945/nprs-history-podcast-throughline-explores-policing-in-america

Video

www.npr.org/2020/07/08/888174033/video-history-of-policing-how-did-we-get-here

Activity Two

(1) Discuss your thoughts on human rights and the history of American policing.

In your discussion, you might consider addressing the following:

A. What do you think about the history of American policing and its relationship to human rights?
B. Do you agree or disagree with any of the rights or facts presented about the history of American policing? If so, provide examples and explain.
C. Is it possible to resolve any contradictions that might exist between human rights and policing? If so, how? Examples?
D. Do you believe any of these potential contradictions exist today? Why or why not? Explain.
E. Freely and openly share your thoughts about the topic using good examples to illustrate any points. Remember, the goal is for everyone in this class to enjoy the conversations, discuss some critical ideas, expose ourselves to different thoughts, and find some stimulation in discussion.

Notes

1 As will be discussed in Chapter 2 on the evolution of human rights, while human rights exists as a concept, and a relatively new one in human civilization, human rights is not widely practiced in reality.
2 As will be discussed in Chapter 3, folk devils arise from media-created moral panics where certain groups of people are stigmatized and scapegoated to blame for large structural problems.
3 According to the Institute for Policy Studies, "Over the last 14 months of the pandemic, millions of Americans have lost their jobs, health and wealth—and almost 600,000 have lost their lives. At the same time, U.S. billionaires and the super-rich have seen their wealth surge to democracy-distorting levels. Between March 18, 2020 and April 15, 2021, the combined wealth of U.S. billionaires increased by $1.6 trillion, a 55 percent increase." *Billionaire Pandemic Wealth Gains of 55% or 1.6 Trillion, Come Amid Three Decades of Rapid Wealth Growth*. Institute for Policy Studies, n.d. Retrieved at: https://inequality.org/wp-content/uploads/2021/04/IPS-ATF-Billionaires-13-Month-31-Year-Report-copy.pdf.
4 Some people would argue that non-human animals should also enjoy these same human rights.

References

Greenwald, Glenn. 2021. "The Journalistic Tattletale and Censorship Industry Suffers Several Well-Deserved Blows." https://greenwald.substack.com/p/the-journalistic-tattletale-and-censorship?utm_campaign=post&utm_medium=web.

United Nations. 1948. Universal Declaration of Human Rights. www.un.org/en/about-us/universal-declaration-of-human-rights

Chapter 2

Connecting Human Rights to Policing

> As I write, highly civilized human beings are flying overhead, trying to kill me. They do not feel any enmity against me as an individual, nor I against them. They are "only doing their duty," as the saying goes. Most of them, I have no doubt, are kind-hearted law-abiding men who would never dream of committing murder in private life.
>
> (George Orwell, The Lion and the Unicorn: Socialism and the English Genius)

Introduction

Police officers prevent people from enjoying their human rights every day.[1] This is not an antagonistic statement, but rather one of objective fact. Police officers, to perform their duties, must restrict people they serve from enjoying their human rights. Police officers often have good, and legal, reasons to restrict the enjoyment of human rights, but nonetheless, they restrict human rights enjoyments all the same. The purpose of this book on human rights policing is not to stop police officers from preventing people from enjoying their human rights when necessary. Rather, the purpose is to help police think about which human rights they will allow the people they serve to enjoy, or which rights they will deny them.

This chapter discusses the three types of policing social interactions in order to begin thinking about how to apply human rights to all of your interactions with community members. It is essential to note that human rights policing is not just about treating people equally, showing empathy and compassion, being nice and kind, giving respect and dignity to people, or being racially and culturally sensitive and aware. Of course we should all do those things. That's not special. That's the bare minimum. We are all supposed to be good, caring, loving, compassionate people.

Those things are important, but human rights policing goes beyond that. Chapter 2 demonstrates how police officers can allow community members to enjoy as many possible human rights that belong to them throughout your entire police interaction with community members. This discussion, and later in the chapter, your application of human rights policing to the three types of policing social interactions will begin the process of applying human rights to police work.

This chapter further discusses the meaning of human rights, as well as its evolution, before arriving at the importance of the United Nations Declaration of Human Rights. We further analyze the United Nations Declaration of Human Rights from the perspectives of police officers as well as from both authors' personal experiences, including anecdotal stories from real-life policing situations to showcase how to apply human rights to everyday policing. Various police officers make contributions discussing their favorite, or most important human rights, and interpret their meanings related to policing. In the end, we ask you to apply what

DOI: 10.4324/9781003220282-3

you learned in the chapter to give examples of the three types of police social interactions and to discuss three human rights, including those you find most important to policing, your interpretation of those rights, and why you find them most important to policing.

Cops of the World, Unite (Under Human Rights Policing)!

In the social sciences, some scholars give a prescriptive account of human behavior discussing some aspect of social reality. These prescriptive accounts focus not on "what is" but rather how things ought to be in their preconceived world, that is, the way they think the world ought to become. Other social scientists provide a more descriptive account of social phenomenon attempting to provide a more objective, actual account of social life. Descriptive accounts discuss what is and, often, provide an explanation, usually why or how, of what is. In this book, we offer both a prescriptive and descriptive account of policing and human rights. The approach, *prima facie*, might surprise the reader.

As law enforcement agents and police officers, you prevent people from enjoying their human rights every day. Police officers may have good, and often legal, reasons to restrict human rights, but nonetheless, they restrict human rights as a matter of objective fact. It is their inevitable job to prevent people from enjoying their human rights, cops have no other choice if they wish to fulfill their obligations as a police officer. As police officers, you prevent the enjoyment of a human's human rights in many community interactions that require police action. For example, police officers restrict a person's freedom even when they stop someone for questioning, pull him over for a traffic violation, or briefly detain her for further investigation. Police also threaten to take away people's freedom for much longer periods of time for more legally egregious offenses. When police arrest someone, it's a social degradation ceremony that takes away a person's feelings of dignity, respect, and honor in front of those witnessing the arrest, either in person, or in print or social media. In short, getting arrested is a humiliating experience that prevents a person from enjoying their human rights, whether deserving or not. When police use force on someone, they touch his body and use their strength and power to dominate another human against her will. When police frisk another human, they put their hands all over another person's body, violate her privacy, strip him of dignity. Though it's not the fault of individual police officers, even their presence with guns, tasers, truncheons, chemical sprays, handcuffs, and other such instruments capable of violence threaten feelings of safety and security for some people.

In short, as police officers, you restrict people from enjoying their human rights all the time, and, if you wish to remain in law enforcement, you will continue to do so in fulfillment of your duties as police officers. Our goal for human rights policing, on the other hand, is prescriptive in the sense that we believe human-rights-focused policing can improve the nature of law enforcement, and thereby improve the health and vitality of our communities.

We want you to realize, or better, fully become aware of how, and when, you restrict the human rights of the people you police in your community. At this point you must decide: "Which human rights will I decide to restrict, and not restrict, in all my interactions with members of the community?" *This is the essence of human rights policing: to become fully aware, or hyper-conscious, of your restrictions of an individual's human rights and realizing your ability to decide with purposive, active, conscious intent, which human rights you will allow members of the community to enjoy, or not enjoy, in your interactions with each member of the community while doing police work.* We argue that the greatest demonstration of human rights policing is when law enforcement agents focus on protecting, as best as possible, and even in the most inconvenient of situations, human rights that they may have otherwise restricted without first becoming fully aware of human rights policing.

Human Rights: Words Without Meaning, Bark Without Bite

Nowadays, words seem stripped of meaning and substance. Worse, people increasingly find words useful in their ability to obscure action and intent, conceal thoughts, and hide the meaning behind action. Politicians, journalists, academics, and other professionals find utility in language to virtue signal righteousness and boast of possessing the "correct" views and attitudes, without any real attempt to fight for a better society.

In today's highly divided world, the dubious relationship between language and politics rears its ugly head. But with closer inspection of the use of language, using a critical discourse analysis, we can see how politicians, academics, corporatists, and journalists use words to hide meaning, manipulate thought, and obscure reality. In his critique of the debasement of language in politics, English writer and philosopher George Orwell argues that writers, academics, politicians, and propagandists intend to make words vague and meaningless to hide the truth, not express it. As Orwell nicely puts it, "Prose consists less and less of words chosen for the sake of their meaning, and more and more of phrases tacked together like the sections of a prefabricated hen-house." In his continued critique of the debasement of language in politics, Orwell states:

> The word *fascism* has now no meaning except in so far as it signifies "something not desirable." The words *democracy, socialism, freedom, patriotic, realistic, justice,* have each of them several different meanings which cannot be reconciled with one another. In the case of a word like *democracy,* not only is there no agreed definition, but the attempt to make one is resisted from all sides. It is almost universally felt that when we call a country democratic we are praising it: Consequently the defenders of every kind of regime claim that it is a democracy, and fear that they might have to stop using the word if it were tied down to any one meaning. Words of this kind are often used in a consciously dishonest way. That is, the person who uses them has his own private definition, but allows his hearer to think he means something quite different. Statements like *Marshal Pétain was a true patriot. The Soviet Press is the freest in the world. The Catholic Church is opposed to persecution,* are almost always made with the intent to deceive. Others words used in variable meanings, in most cases more or less dishonestly, are: *class, totalitarian, science, progressive, reactionary, bourgeois, equality.*
>
> (Orwell 2013)

Has the use of the words "human rights" fallen into such meaninglessness and vagary as democracy, fascism, communism, patriotism, tolerance, justice, empathy, and equity? Has the meaning and understanding of human rights, still, as will be explained below, a concept in its infancy in relation to human civilization, become increasingly obscured with intentional misuse of the term? George Orwell could have easily included human rights within his list of words so misused today.

Such popular words used today such as equity, inclusion, anti-racism, tolerance, empathy, empowerment, patriotism, social justice, equality, democracy, and, of course, human rights, sound good, but how are they used to justify and, at other times, conceal contemptible behaviors? Or in the words of the great gonzo journalist Hunter S. Thompson, "Freedom, Truth, Honour you could rattle off a hundred such words and behind every one of them would gather a thousand punks, pompous little farts, waving the banner with one hand and reaching under the table with the other" (1999). While many people in professional positions (academics, politicians, police officers, judges, and so on) frequently virtue signal to symbolically demonstrate their possession of the culturally "correct" thoughts and attitudes of the time, perhaps the singer-song writer Phil Ochs' *Love me I'm a Liberal*[2] captures such virtue signaling best.

While almost everyone symbolically agrees with the concept of human rights, and certainly knows that they are *supposed* to outwardly agree with human rights to signal the culturally correct attitudes, most people's actions fall well short of their symbolic representation. Nation-states drop their "freedom bombs" in the name of human rights. Politicians allow corporations to rig elections and write social policy in the name of freedom and human rights. Militarily powerful countries invade militarily weaker, autonomous countries all the time, sometimes in the name of human rights. Or as Orwell stated, language "is designed to make lies sound truthful and murder respectable, and to give an appearance of solidity to pure wind" (2013/1946).

Many academics, despite their rhetoric, use the same oppressive hierarchical institutions they purport to be against to exert power and control over colleagues using the virtue signaling words such as inclusivity, social justice, and equity. Similarly, police officers, at times, use moral and righteous justifications to explain behavior that gives much of the world a sense of pause and disquiet. In other words, no one is immune to contradiction, misusing words for careerism or personal gain, virtue signaling, and outright justifying contemptible behavior. That's why we call for a clear understanding of human rights and its application toward policing.

How do we understand the concept of human rights when governments, political parties, human rights groups, charities, academics, economists, urban planners, and scores of other professional and political groups frequently use the term as political rhetoric to conceal meaning in an era of language debasement?

We start with the idea that human rights policing must go beyond something nice to put on one's resume. It must go beyond demonstrating to the public and those in your field that you *theoretically* hold the correct cultural ideas because you incorporate the right empty, ephemeral political buzzwords into the party line in polite conversations. The words we use only have meaning when actions back them up. If you take these ideas to heart, human rights policing is something that you can materialize, that you can make *real* in your community. Materializing human rights policing into reality, that is, actions, requires clearly understanding the concrete rights humans inherently possess, and further, implementing a consistent practice of recognizing and making sure that the people you protect and serve enjoy, to the fullest extent possible, all of the human rights that naturally belong to them.

The next two sections attempt to provide more clarity on the concept of human rights, the definition and meaning of human rights, and its evolution throughout history. We connect our understanding of human rights to the field of policing. We offer law enforcement agents new ways of thinking about human rights as it relates to police work.

The Nature and Meaning of Human Rights

Human rights are universal rights belonging to all humans throughout time and space simply because of their membership to the *Homo sapiens* species. Although important in all our social interactions, human rights go beyond the concept of doing the right thing, or treating people nicely or with kindness, or even respecting government-ordained civil rights. They also go beyond treating people with respect. Rather, human rights imply entitlement, something that is owed to human beings simply because they are humans (Donnelly 2013). It is the highest right, above the law and transcends the moral, ethical, or legal authority of any private or governmental body, group, or organization. Human rights exist equally for all humans regardless of their legal status, nationality, race, ethnicity, sex, gender, or any other socially prescribed category. Human rights also exist equally to all humans regardless of the character, nature, ability, or behavior. As the scholar Donnelly puts it:

> Human rights are equal rights: one either is or is not a human being, and therefore has the same human rights as everyone else (or none at all). Human rights also are inalienable rights: one cannot stop being human, no matter how badly one behaves or how barbarously one is treated. And they are universal rights, in the sense that today we consider all members of the species Homo sapiens "human beings" and thus holders of human rights.
> (Donnelly 2013)

Donnelly distinguishes between three major forms of social interaction involving rights:

1. "Assertive exercise": the right is exercised (asserted, claimed, pressed), activating the obligations of the duty-bearer, who then either respects the right or violates it (in which case he is liable to enforcement action).
2. "Active respect": the duty-bearer takes the right into account in determining how to behave, without the right-holder ever claiming it. The right has been respected and enjoyed, even though it has not been actively exercised. Enforcement may have been considered by the duty-bearer but is otherwise out of the picture.
3. "Objective enjoyment": rights apparently never enter the transaction, … neither right-holder nor duty-bearer gives them any thought. The right—or at least the object of the right—has been enjoyed. Ordinarily, though, we would not say that it has been respected, and neither exercise nor enforcement is in any way involved.

Of course, as Donnelly states, "In an ideal world, rights would remain both out of sight and out of mind" (2013). That is, they would appear natural, normal, and in evitable for people to enjoy. In our case, police would naturally allow people to enjoy the human rights that belong to them all the time except when absolutely necessary to keep the individual and community safe.

Three Types of Human Rights Policing Social Interactions

For the purposes of law enforcement agents, police officers serve as the duty-bearers responsible for respecting (upholding) the human rights of the right-holders—members of the community being policed. It is up to police officers, as duty-bearers, to make sure that members of the community, right-holders, enjoy their human rights to the maximum degree possible.

Borrowing from Donnelly, we develop what we call the "Three Types of Human Rights Policing Social Interactions" to describe police officer interactions with members of the community as it relates human rights policing.

1. *Assertive Exercise Police Interactions*: A police officer listens to a community member exercise, or state, his human rights in the process of a police interaction. The police officer is now notified of the claim to human rights being expressed by the community member. The police officer must now decide to respect, violate, or restrict the human rights of the community member.
2. *Active Respect Police Interactions*: In the course of interacting with a community member(s), the police officer recognizes, without any claim to human rights by the community member, the various human rights of the community member. The police officer respects all of the human rights of the community member unless it becomes impossible to fully

respect all of her human rights. In such cases, the police officer only restricts the human rights of the individual in order to successfully fulfill one's duty and keep everyone safe. In most cases, the hope is that the police officer fosters a scene where community members enjoy all of their human rights, that is, the police officer respects all of the human rights in the police interaction.

3. *Objective Enjoyment Police Interactions*: The police officer "naturally" respects the human rights of the community member as a matter of common sense and mutual respect. The police interaction goes so well that the community member never even thinks to express their claim to human rights due to the police officer's ability to naturally respect the human rights of all people she interacts with in the course of doing police work.

In all of these police interactions with community members, the fulfillment of human rights always depends on the police officer—the dependent variable in the equation. The community member, the independent variable, is always in possession of human rights, whether or not she states (exercises) her rights, remains acutely aware of these rights, or doesn't think about her rights at all. Donnelly develops the concept of the "possession paradox" to describe "'having' and 'not having' a right at the same time—possessing it but not enjoying it—with the 'having' being particularly important precisely when one does not 'have' it'" (2013, 9). In our case related to human rights policing, the "possession paradox" explains how the community member, right-holder, both possesses and does not possess human rights. Every community member possesses human rights but does not enjoy (possess the object) their human rights unless the police officer both consciously recognizes and actively respects those rights. The community member being policed always *has* the right, again whether he states it or not, but does not *enjoy* the right he possesses unless the police officer respects the right during the entire policing interaction process. As a result, the police officer decides which rights the possessor of human rights enjoys. The police officer must remain, at all times, highly aware of all the human rights community members possess, and decide to respect those rights, restrict those rights, or deny and violate those rights to the right-holder.

Protecting the enjoyment of human rights goes beyond abstract ideas, virtue signaling, symbolic expressions, or justifications to hide behind. We want you to think of human rights not so much as a noun but a verb, a conscious action, a specific set of behaviors actively carried out in all your interactions with the community. Yes, human rights are values, an ideal, a powerful concept, but they mean nothing unless you, as police officers—duty-bearers—become fully aware and actively respect, to the highest degree possible, all of the human rights of the people you police. Human rights policing focuses on law enforcement agents protecting the enjoyment of human rights, to the fullest extent possible, for everyone in the community.

Examples of the Three Human Rights Policing Social Interactions

The second author provides some simple examples below of each type of policing social interaction taken from first-hand experiences serving in the New Orleans Police Department.

Example One: Assertive Exercise Police Interactions

I was working in the Third Police District in a two-person car when my partners and I received a call of a family disturbance in our area. We responded to the call, arrived at the destination, and knocked on the door of the address dispatch provided. A man about six feet four inches tall and weighing probably in excess of 250 pounds answered the door and invited us inside saying that he did not call the police. It was his wife, he stated, who called us. As we looked around, we saw a woman sitting in the living room crying. The woman told us that she and her husband had been arguing and that he hit her in the head. She was afraid he would hit her again if he remained in the house. The man intervened, admitting that he hit her because he got so angry. At that point my partner and I agreed that the best course of action was to arrest the man to protect the woman from potential harm. In order to perform our duties, it became necessary to temporarily prevent this man from enjoying all of his human rights. Further, removing him from the house would allow a court intervention to help keep the woman safe, and potentially help the couple with their marriage. I approached the man and advised him that he was under arrest for simple battery on his wife. He responded immediately, saying that he understood and would go willingly. He then added that he knew his rights, that we needed to read him his Miranda rights, and that we could not abuse him in any way or prevent him from enjoying all the human rights that belong to him.

I was a little surprised about his demand.

I told him that we would do that and that we had no intention of harming him. The last time he got arrested, he said, the officers pushed and struck him due to his size. He added that was not going to happen again because he knew his rights, and further knew that police officers cannot mistreat or abuse him in any way, including unnecessarily preventing him from enjoying his human rights. Since he was so large, we handcuffed him using two pairs of handcuffs as one pair did not reach both wrists. We informed the woman that we would have someone contact her from a battered women's organization and left the house with the man. We placed the man in the rear seat of our police car, seat belted him, and proceeded to the lock-up where we turned him over to the Sheriff's office personnel. Finally, as we were departing, he looked at us and asked, "I get a phone call, right?" I asked the deputy to make sure he got his phone call. While it became necessary to prevent this man from enjoying all of his human rights to perform our duties as law enforcement agents, and to protect the wife from potential harm, we also made sure that this man could enjoy as many of his human rights as possible during our entire interaction. He certainly understood his rights, and we learned to appreciate community members who express their rights to us in all of our policing social interactions.

Example Two: Active Respect Police Interactions

While working a one-person car in the Second Police District, I received a call of a shoplifting incident at a large retail store. I proceeded to the store and was directed to the personnel office where two store detectives were holding a man who, they indicated, attempted to shoplift a set of tools worth $75.00 in US currency. The detectives added that they observed the man place a small tool box in his jacket pocket, followed him as he passed the checkouts, and stopped him in the parking lot. They showed me the toolbox in question. I instructed the detectives to keep the toolbox for evidence and that they would receive a subpoena requiring them to be in court with the evidence. I turned to the man in question, advised him that he was under arrest for shoplifting, took off the detective's handcuffs, and replaced them with mine. I escorted the man to my police car in the parking lot, placed him in the back, and proceeded to ask him some questions in order to fill out my report. When I asked for his name, he gave it to me, stating, "Officer, I have a job in a local warehouse, if I don't show up this afternoon, they are going to fire me." I replied that if he knew that why did he try to steal the tool box. He told me that his car had a mechanical problem that he could fix, he just didn't have the tools or the money to buy them. He said that he knew he was wrong, but that he was desperate as he needed his car to get to work.

Based on what I learned from this man, I decided to exercise my option to write him a summons to appear in court the next day in lieu of a physical arrest. I realized that it was unnecessary to prevent this man from enjoying his human rights in light of the fact that I had the summons option. I took him out of the rear of the police car, removed the handcuffs, and asked him to sign the affidavit for the summons. I drove him to his car and released him with the understanding that he was not to come back to this store, at least until the shoplifting case was adjudicated in Municipal Court.

This was a case in which I had the chance to allow a member of the community the opportunity to enjoy all his human rights while at the same time performing my duties as a police officer that hold the man accountable for his actions.

Example Three: Objective Enjoyment Police Interactions

Over many years serving my community as a police officer, I always looked at my role not just as the protector of human rights, but as the enforcer of human rights. That is not to say that I did not prevent people from enjoying their human rights. I certainly made hundreds, if not thousands, of arrests for many illegal actions during my career. Many of those arrests were based on the safety of the community. I can cite many incidents in which I was able, as a natural way of doing police work, to allow community members to enjoy all their human rights, including the right to liberty. For example, when patrolling an area of the city late one night, I observed a young man making an illegal left turn. I stopped the vehicle and asked the young man, 18 years old, to exit the car. The youngster exited the car and approached me asking what was wrong. Smelling the odor of alcohol, I asked him where he was coming from tonight. He replied that he recently left his girlfriend's house where he drank a beer with the women's parents after dinner. He added that he was going to college and lived with his parents not far away from our location. I ran his name through our computers and found no current warrants for his arrest. The young man did not appear intoxicated as I checked him walking and talking. Still, he had made an illegal left turn. At that point, I asked him to use the phone to dial his parents' phone number and turn the phone over to me. After a few rings, a man who later identified himself as the father answered the phone. I explained to him the situation and asked to verify the story the young man told me. The father said that yes, his son had been invited to his girlfriend's house for dinner and that he knew the family well, and further, that his son does not drink alcohol excessively. Finally, the man asked if I could just detain his son until he could pick him up just to be sure that the young man could get home safely. I evaluated the situation based on the young man being honest with me, including drinking a beer. Further, his father, willing to pick up his son, verified his story. Finally, he did not appear intoxicated and was not wanted for any law violations. Based on that information, I decided to allow him to enjoy all of his human rights and allowed his father to pick him up to take him home. This was a case in which both parties expected all human rights to be respected without even mentioning the subject.

A brief look into the history of human rights might provide a deeper appreciation for the concept and its application toward today's world, especially policing.

Evolution of Human Rights

Universal human rights—defined as "equal and inalienable rights that all human beings have simply because they are human and that they may exercise against their own state and society"—emerged as a concept, but far from a reality, in the middle of the sixteenth century (Donnelly 2013, 75).[3] While the concept of universal human rights emerged relatively recently in human history, the actual practice of human rights developed, arguably, in the late 20th century. Various scholars have argued that universal human rights emerged in earlier human civilizations, but such claims fall well short of the definitional standards of the concept. While other civilizations in the premodern world throughout traditional China, traditional Africa, Islam, classical Greece, and Medieval Europe displayed various forms of social justice, individual rights, monarchal divine obligations to citizens, codes of ethics regarding personal dignity and worth, rights to justice and freedom, economic rights, rulership for the common good, and limited government, individual worth was always dependent upon achievement, status, age, sex, tribal affiliation, lineage, responsibility, land ownership, or some other attribute tied to the individual (Donnelly 2013). In other words, until recently in human history, there was no concept that every human being possessed equal and inalienable rights simply because they are human. As Donnelly puts it, "Such rights were not human rights. They had to be earned. They could be lost. Their ground was not the fact that one was a human being. The dignity and worth in question were not inalienable and inherent" (2013, 77). Many of the individual rights and protections individuals enjoyed derived often from divine commandments, religious authority, monarchal obligations to citizenry, governmental balances of power, limited government, traditional values and beliefs, rights and duties of community membership, but never from the ability of a person to claim a right against a society or government simply because she is a member of a particular species.

In Ancient Greece, a time and place some proclaim the first bastion of democracy, such democratic enjoyment included only the wealthy and privileged, usually based on birth right, land ownership, or access to a military. The ancient Greeks developed the concept of individual rights within the ideological ranking system centered around hierarchy. Plato's *the Great Chain of Being* formalized the ideology of "natural" hierarchy and access to rights: first Greek men, then non-Greek men, women, slaves, and last, non-human animals (Lovejoy 1936). Those higher within the hierarchy received greater rights and freedoms than those lower in the chain. Some observers argue that not much seems to have fundamentally changed in human society, despite much of our rhetoric.

While the Greeks unevenly divided rights between Greeks and outsider "barbarians," Medieval Europe did so between Christians and "heathens" (Donnelly 2013). Just as in Greece's "natural" hierarchy, Medieval Europe organized itself with extreme religious and secular hierarchies that unequally granted rights and privileges based on one's position within the social stratum. Of course, the religious crusades showcased some of the most heinous acts of brutal violence providing further evidence that human rights only belonged to certain groups. In short, for both Ancient Greek and Medieval Europe, "hierarchy and division, rather than any shared sense of a common humanity or equal rights, dominated political thought and practice" (Donnelly 2013, 84).

Much of European history remained just as hierarchal as its earlier history, complete with the divine rights of kings and rights belonging mainly to people in the upper echelons of the social hierarchy based on birthright, and later, property ownership. After the bloody Hundred Years War, early modern Europe continued its savagely brutal and violent ways with peasant wars, religious wars and massacres, including the Thirty Years War and the English Civil War, among others, making any notion of human rights far from a political, ethical, or moral concept, much less a reality (Donnelly 2013). Society remained based on a hierarchal institutional arrangement that justified elite rule, slavery, patriarchy, subordination, and domination. In short, universal human rights, both as an idea and practice, did not exist.

The great structural transformations of modernity brought about radical political, social, cultural, economic, and religious transformations that disrupted the fabric of social life.

Modernity arose from the ashes of feudalism, bringing about the advent of a mercantilist economic system leading to a bourgeoise capitalistic system based around the notion of a newly emerging nation-state with defined borders, political autonomy, and a monopoly on the means of violence. Capitalistic markets and a bureaucratic state broke free of conceptions of divine right and religious authority, replacing such notions with alternative hierarchical forms that claimed to be more egalitarian, democratic, and free. But the great structural changes brought about a loosening of the moorings for the masses where social life becomes disrupted as the bonds holding society together disintegrate. For many, radical social change brought about nomic ruptures, that is, erosion of community efficacy and bonds, fractures in hegemony, and a crisis of institutional legitimacy, creating a precarious world in constant motion. As Donnelly puts it, "In the process, 'traditional' communities, and their systems of mutual support and obligation, were disrupted, destroyed, or radically transformed, typically with traumatic consequences" (2013, 87). The disruption of political, social, economic, and religious life also brought about possibilities for change, including physical and social mobility from which the beginnings of the notion of human rights emerged. People began to demand political, social, and economic inclusion into the social order, their right to stake a claim in the world. Donnelly says, "such demands took many forms, including appeals to scripture, church, morality, tradition, justice, natural law, order, social utility, and national strength. Claims of equal and inalienable natural or human rights, however, increasingly came to be preferred—and over the past couple decades have become globally hegemonic" (2013, 87). It should be noted, however, that individual rights, even during the heightened ideas of the enlightenment, applied mainly to white wealthy men, not women, "barbarian" outsiders, slaves, servants, wage laborers, or the poor.

While some well-known documents throughout Western history, such as the Magna Carta (1215) and the English Bill of Rights (1689), discussed rights and liberties, it was based on belonging to a group or country, for example Englishmen, and, further, appeals to authority still relied on notions of divine right and responsibility to the governed. The United States 1776 Declaration of Independence (and later the 1791 Bill of Rights) and the French Declaration on the Rights of Man and Citizen (1789) provided perhaps the first real expression of unalienable, "natural" human rights that apply equally to all humans. The French took the concept even further, stating that the violation of human rights serves as the primary cause of social disruption, discontent, and corruption (Donnelly 2013). Of course, while these ideas existed, they still only applied to rich white men, largely excluding women, the poor, propertyless, slaves, the colonized, racialized groups, and manufactured folk devils (see Chapter 3), among many others. Human civilization still had a long way to go, and still does, to achieve universal rights for all humans.

Fast forward to the nineteenth century where human civilizations witnessed the evils of the genocide of indigenous peoples, colonialism, racial slavery, indentured servitude, apartheid, race-based internment camps, and industrial wage slavery; and fast forwarding through history a bit more, to the twentieth century where the human race saw the horrors of WWI, Nazi Germany and the holocaust, WWII, and US colonizing campaigns throughout Latin America, among many other wars. The shock of the past two centuries indicated to some observers that something had to be done about human rights.

For the continuation of human civilization and the ongoing human experiment of democracy, the Western world realized that rights must become universal, applied to all human beings regardless of their socially prescribed categories based on race, ethnicity, sex, gender, religion, language, political affiliation, or any other manufactured quality. Enter the Declaration of Human Rights.

The United Nations Declaration of Human Rights

In the aftermath of WWII, the United Nations General Assembly gathered in Paris on December 10, 1948 to proclaim the first ever articulation of human rights for the universal protection of every human on earth, now widely known as the Universal Declaration of Human Rights (United Nations, 1948). The Universal Declaration became the most translated document in the world (525 languages at the time of this writing) and today serves as an inspiration to both old and newly emerging democracies. According to the United Nations, representatives from different legal and cultural backgrounds from every region on the earth drafted the document that now defines "a common standard of achievements for all peoples and all nations" (Ibid).

The United Nations defines human rights as

> rights inherent to all human beings, regardless of income, class, race, sex, nationality, ethnicity, language, religion, or any other status. Human rights include the right to life and liberty, freedom from slavery and torture, freedom of opinion and expression, the right to work and education, and many more. Everyone is entitled to these rights, without discrimination.
>
> (Ibid)

The Declaration of Human Rights, as the preamble states, emerged from the "disregard and contempt for human rights (that) have resulted in barbarous acts which have outraged the conscience of mankind." The Preamble of The Declaration of Human Rights, stated at length below, uses language such as inherent dignity, equal and inalienable rights, freedom and justice, peace, freedom of speech and belief, freedom from fear, dignity and worth to apply to all of the members of the human family—*Homo sapiens*—and, further, states that when such rights are infringed, human beings have the right to rebel against that tyranny and oppression. It's a radical document for the human species, a concept relatively new to human civilization, and an alternative path forward to course a new path in human history. While we now have the concept of human rights, we remain far from realizing it in practice throughout the world. It's worth a read.[4]

> Whereas recognition of the inherent dignity and of the equal and inalienable rights of all members of the human family is the foundation of freedom, justice and peace in the world,
>
> Whereas disregard and contempt for human rights have resulted in barbarous acts which have outraged the conscience of mankind, and the advent of a world in which human beings shall enjoy freedom of speech and belief and freedom from fear and want has been proclaimed as the highest aspiration of the common people,
>
> Whereas it is essential, if man is not to be compelled to have recourse, as a last resort, to rebellion against tyranny and oppression, that human rights should be protected by the rule of law,
>
> Whereas it is essential to promote the development of friendly relations between nations,
>
> Whereas the peoples of the United Nations have in the Charter reaffirmed their faith in fundamental human rights, in the dignity and worth of the human person and in the equal rights of men and women and have determined to promote social progress and better standards of life in larger freedom,

Whereas Member States have pledged themselves to achieve, in co-operation with the United Nations, the promotion of universal respect for and observance of human rights and fundamental freedoms,

Whereas a common understanding of these rights and freedoms is of the greatest importance for the full realization of this pledge,

Now, Therefore THE GENERAL ASSEMBLY proclaims THIS UNIVERSAL DECLARATION OF HUMAN RIGHTS as a common standard of achievement for all peoples and all nations, to the end that every individual and every organ of society, keeping this Declaration constantly in mind, shall strive by teaching and education to promote respect for these rights and freedoms and by progressive measures, national and international, to secure their universal and effective recognition and observance, both among the peoples of Member States themselves and among the peoples of territories under their jurisdiction

(Ibid)

Thirty articles follow the preamble articulating the meaning of human rights as it applies to dignity, freedom, rights, life, liberty, security, treatment, recognition, health, status, travel, and so on that applies to all human beings regardless of race, class, gender, ethnicity, citizenship, legal status, documentation, or any other consideration (United Nations, 1948).[5] Use footnote ten to read all 30 articles. Shortly, in a section below, we will provide brief passages from current and retired police officers and law enforcement agents discussing what human rights they find most important to policing, their interpretation of those rights, and why they find them most important to policing.

International Covenant on Civil and Political Rights

Years later, the United Nations General Assembly ratified (1966) and adopted (1976) the International Covenant on Civil and Political Rights (ICCPR) further expounding upon the civil and political rights of human beings (United Nations 1966).[6] In its preamble, the covenant also uses such language as the "inherent dignity and of the equal and inalienable rights of all members of the human family" and "the inherent dignity of the human person" and "the ideal of free human beings enjoying civil and political freedom and freedom from fear and want" that "can only be achieved if conditions are created whereby everyone may enjoy his civil and political rights, as well as his economic, social and cultural rights." The reader can easily access these universal civil and political rights, Parts I, II, and III (the first 27 Articles) of the ICCPR are most relevant to police officers.

Summary of Human Rights

Although we encourage the reader to read the U.N. Declaration of Human Rights and the ICCPR, we provide a list of the internationally recognized human rights from both documents to provide a clear overview of recognized universal human rights that apply to all people at all times.

Universal Human Rights

Equality of rights without discrimination
Life
Liberty and security of person
Protection against slavery

Protection against torture and cruel and inhuman punishment
Recognition as a person before the law
Equal protection of the law
Access to legal remedies for rights violations
Protection against arbitrary arrest or detention
Hearing before an independent and impartial judiciary
Presumption of innocence
Protection against ex post facto laws
Protection of privacy, family, and home
Freedom of movement and residence
Seek asylum from persecution
Nationality
Marry and found a family
Own property
Freedom of thought, conscience, and religion
Freedom of opinion, expression, and the press
Freedom of assembly and association
Political participation
Social security
Work, under favorable conditions
Free trade unions
Rest and leisure
Food, clothing, and housing
Health care and social services
Special protections for children
Education
Participation in cultural life
A social and international order needed to realize rights
Self-determination
Humane treatment when detained or imprisoned
Protection against debtor's prison
Protection against arbitrary expulsion of aliens
Protection against advocacy of racial or religious hatred
Protection of minority culture

We end this chapter with some contributions from current and former law enforcement agents discussing their views on human rights and policing.

Human Rights from the Perspective of Police Officers

Along with interviewing dozens of police officers, we asked current and retired law enforcement agents from various police departments to discuss their views on human rights and policing. In the passages that follow below, police officers provide their accounts of what human rights they find most important to their jobs, their interpretation of those rights, and why they find them most important to policing. In most situations, police officers chose which human rights they find most important to policing from the 30 articles in the United Nations Declaration of Human Rights and Parts I, II, and III, or the first 27 articles, of the International Covenant on Civil and Political Rights. The second author, a 30-year veteran on the New Orleans Police Department, provides the first response.

Lt. Pedro Marina (Retired)

Article 6, International Covenant on Civil and Political Rights is unquestionably one of the most important rights as it has to do with the right to life. It reads, "Every human being has the inherent right to life. This right shall be protected by law. No one shall be arbitrarily deprived of his life." This article can be problematic for any human being facing a threat to his or her life, but it is of particular importance for police officers as they constantly carry a firearm with the ability to kill.

Police officers often confront life-threatening situations that require the use of deadly force. This human right would not be as much of a problem for a soldier in a war zone gunfight. But, for police officers operating in their community, the right to life is more challenging.

I'll explain my view.

Our economic system creates a highly unequal society with large pockets of poverty in most, if not all, of our cities. As police officers, we operate in these communities with poverty and high degrees of relative deprivation, and, often, more crime. We are more likely to stop and question people in those communities than in the more affluent parts of the city. With that in mind, we must be aware of putting ourselves or the people in those less affluent communities at risk of the use of deadly force. We must "serve and protect" these communities as any other community in our city. The people in these communities deserve equal treatment because they are human beings with inherent rights as everyone else. Further, as we work there, we have to be aware of those unfair inequalities and our responses to them.

Article 10, International Covenant on Civil and Political Rights states that "all persons deprived of their liberty shall be treated with humanity and with respect for the inherent dignity of the human person." As police officers, we have the power, indeed, the requirement, of depriving citizens of their freedom. What a responsibility! That is why it is so important to adhere to the exact text of article 10: to treat those we arrest with "humanity and respect for the inherent dignity of the human person." There were many times when I made an arrest, especially for a felony involving a victim, when I felt sorry and compassion not just for the victim, but also for the perpetrator. Of course, the victims suffer, and their life becomes irrevocably altered often due to situations beyond their control. We must recognize that. We must also recognize that the perpetrator's life is also altered, even if he intentionally commits the crime. The perpetrator potentially faces years locked away in prison—certainly a ruined life. As we discussed in this chapter, we don't always know the structural conditions that cause the personal troubles people face, and we have not walked in their shoes. What's more, the perpetrator, regardless of the act committed, retains full possession of his human rights. Our job is to make sure he enjoys his human rights even after committing acts we might despise.

Article 9, International Covenant on Civil and Political Rights states that "everyone has the right to liberty and security of person. No one shall be subjected to arbitrary arrest or detention. No one shall be deprived of his liberty except on such grounds and in accordance with such procedure as are established by law." It also states that "anyone who is arrested shall be informed, at the time of arrest, of the reasons for his arrest and shall be promptly informed of any charges against him." This particular human right applies mostly to law enforcement. It's a huge part of what we do on a daily basis. Specifically, our approach to anyone in the conduct of a criminal investigation must be based on law and reasonable suspicion. We must be able to articulate that suspicion before we take any action. We cannot just go to any citizen, detain him or her without that reasonable suspicion. If that stop based on reasonable suspicion leads to an arrest, that arrest has to be made on probable cause that the law mandates. The officer must articulate that probable cause before the arrest. And, of course, once the arrest takes place, the officer has the duty to inform the arrestee immediately of the reason for the arrest as well as his Miranda rights against self-incrimination. All those actions, based on constitutional law, are stated in Article 9.

But, what about human "right to liberty and security of person."

As police officers we are called upon to make arrests, that is, to deprive someone of his liberty. When we do that, we must be aware of what that person may be going through at the prospect of what he or she will have to endure at least for some time.

Getting arrested can be a terrifying experience.

The police officer is called upon to show empathy and compassion. The officer needs to explain the process in order to calm some of that fear, terror, and confusion. What's more, if there is anything we can do for the person being arrested that is legal, safe, and permissible by department regulation, we must allow it. It might be as simple as allowing a phone call, or notifying a neighbor, or arranging for the care of children.

We must try to help.

We must keep in mind that an arrest, the taking away of someone's liberty, is a radical action that often is not as radical as the infraction committed by the individual in question.

We can take someone's liberty, but we cannot take away his "right to liberty and security." When we take that radical action of making an arrest that deprives a human of his enjoyment to the human right of liberty, we must be sure that we act in total accordance with law and, just as important, with great dignity, empathy, and compassion.

Chief Roland Camacho

(Chief Roland Camacho offers his views below on human rights and policing. Camacho is a law enforcement executive who spent time as an advisor in Afghanistan and Mexico. He is a graduate of the FBI National Academy, has a master's in Criminal Justice from Liberty University, and is the chief of the Chambersburg Pennsylvania Police Department).

The sixth-century BCE founder and ruler of the Persian empire, Cyrus, earned the moniker "the Great" due to his military conquest, the centralized administration of his vast domain, and most significantly, his development of a "Charter of Human Rights" (Forbes and Prevas 2009, 23). The charter was a revolutionary document in antiquity. Rulers during ancient times often enslaved the people they conquered and imposed their own nation's cultural norms upon them. Habitually this forced inclusion and subjugation occurred oppressively and brutally. Cyrus the Great ensured the preservation of the defeated countries' cultures; he welcomed them into the Persian empire with a spirit of compassion and inclusion.

Most importantly, Cyrus guaranteed the individual rights of his subjects, and his charter was one of the documents used as a written precursor to the United Nations Universal Declaration of Human Rights. Amazingly, thousands of years later, we still have problems honoring our fellow citizen's human rights. Unfortunately, the issue of human rights violations is magnified and widely publicized when the police are involved.

The police have a tremendous and vital mandate to protect the citizens we serve, especially their rights. We should not look upon this immense power as a burden. It is a gift, one that needs to be cherished and safeguarded. Article Two of the Universal Declaration of Human Rights states that everyone is entitled to all the rights and freedoms included within the document. There is no distinction due to race, color, sex, language, religion, political opinion, nationality, property, or any other status. A portion of my department's Mission Statement states that we will "serve all people with fairness and respect." The department's culture of service and intensive training guides all of our officers to act with impartiality and compassion at every police-citizen interaction. This philosophy is incredibly successful, and our strong community support validates the methods are working. I know this is the path forward for law enforcement agencies to regain the trust of the community they serve, especially in those areas where that relationship is broken or damaged.

Step one in the process of repairing or regaining the public's trust is a complete understanding that all people have fundamental human rights, and those rights must be protected at all times; nothing else will matter if that is not accomplished. It is not an unattainable goal. With good training and a commitment from all the ranks within a law enforcement agency to evolve, understand, and honor that all people have basic human rights, we can achieve this goal. Evolution will make the profession of policing stronger than ever. As a young rookie police officer in 1995, my patrol sergeant would always say, "Treat people the way you want to be treated." I know similar sayings and advice were uttered to police officers all over the country since the start of the profession. Over time, many of us in the career of policing forgot that "Golden Rule." If it takes going back thousands of years to rediscover and study the lessons of Cyrus the Great, who uncommonly honored and respected human rights, so be it; it is too important a concept to be ignored anymore.

Chief Allen Hill of the University of Wisconsin—La Crosse Police Department

(Chief Allen Hill holds a bachelor's degree in Criminal Justice from Midwestern State University in Texas. He began his law enforcement career in 1989 with the Texas Highway Patrol as a State Trooper. In 2009, he began working for the University of Houston-Clear Lake before coming to the University of Wisconsin—La Crosse in 2019).

In today's turbulent climate in policing, I believe that preserving human dignity, compassion, and professionalism are priority to me when it comes to policing today. More specifically, I find Article 9—*No one shall be subjected to arbitrary arrest, detention, or exile* a high priority on my list. I choose this one because it is something that I have personally experienced less than two years ago.

I interpret this right to mean that no police officer should randomly arrest, detain, or exile another human being under no circumstance. Now, I know this is a very grey and blurry area that is very subjective. Case and point, a random person is sitting in their car and smoking a cigarette. Of course, this random person is non-white, and none other than myself. I had only been in the city for a few months and was at the time living at a rather nice downtown apartment complex. It was winter and my Texas blood was still adjusting to the brisk mid-west winter.

Because it was cold out, I was sitting in my car smoking a cigarette to stay warm. I observed a police car pull up in front of mine, and the officer got out and approached the driver's side window where I was sitting. I rolled down the window as he approached. He identified himself and asked if I was the owner of the vehicle. I told him I was and asked him if everything was ok. He stated that he ran my license plate and knew that I was a resident of the complex based on the license plate return. He then stated that another resident called me in as a suspicious person.

I told the officer that I was reading the news on my phone and smoking a cigarette, and that I was in my car because it was cold outside. He said that he understood and apologized, that he was just responding to the call they received from the resident. I said that I understood that he was just doing his job and not to worry. He thanked me for my cooperation, wished me well, and departed the area.

As I write this, I can feel my ears turning red as it pisses me off once again. As soon as the officer left, I thought to myself, who the hell had the audacity to call me in as "suspicious?" When did it become illegal to sit in your car in a public place and smoke a cigarette? I was fuming to say the least. In this case, I was detained and not free to leave. So, I was detained for no real lawful reason, and stripped of Article 9 rights for simply sitting in my car and smoking a cigarette. Now, I never identified myself to the officer as it wasn't significant and he was professional throughout the entire contact.

For those few minutes of the contact, I was Joe Average citizen and not a police officer. As I reflected on what had happened, I realized that the officer and I had both just experienced racism by proxy. And had I been another minority person, the contact could have ended much differently. I understood why the officer was there, and that he didn't randomly pick me out. But non-law enforcement people don't understand the innerworkings of police departments and the response to "suspicious" people calls.

A few weeks later I shared my story with the police chief of the agency. He was glad to know that his officer handled the call professionally; however, he was not happy with the call itself and agreed that it probably should not have occurred to begin with. We had several discussions about the incident and how we could possibly prevent similar situations from happening. I shared with him that at my previous agency we started asking more questions on these types of calls, that our dispatchers would ask more questions about what was suspicious.

My story is just one of who knows how many happen on a daily basis throughout the nation. And in many cases, the officer who is out there just trying to do their job gets the brunt of the "suspicious" person's frustration of being felt like they have been discriminated against. We can and must do better in law enforcement, and not allow ourselves to be weaponized to do others' dirty work. It has been engrained in law enforcement that we are the protectors, and that we will investigate suspicious things. The problem with this thinking is that suspicious is very subjective, and it can be very difficult to articulate it. But we can ask questions, and if they don't pass the litmus test, then we should not be trying to sniff things out.

In my case, the officer could have simply driven by and not made contact. But we have been taught to make contact because a concerned citizen reported it. So, because a concerned citizen reported it, their concern gets to trump my basic human rights. And because they are concerned, I get to feel humiliated as people pass by and see an officer talking to me in what clearly appears as a police contact.

For a brief moment I experienced those violations of my basic human rights. It shouldn't have happened then, and it shouldn't happen ever. We can and have to do better in policing. No officer at any level in the organization should allow themselves or their department to be weaponized, or be the subject of racism by proxy. We have to take a broader look at our processes, and how we have typically done things over the years. In my opinion, it is not okay to send an officer to a suspicious person call without asking specific questions. Questions like, "What is suspicious about their behavior?" And if their answers don't pass the litmus test, we have to simply tell them that we will not be sending an officer. Sure, some will get mad but that is okay. A citizen getting mad on the phone will not result in an innocent person getting mad at the officer in the field, and will prevent a situation from turning badly or deadly.

Suggested Readings and Activities

Readings

The United Nations Declaration of Human Rights (www.un.org/en/about-us/universal-declaration-of-human-rights).

The International Covenant on Civil and Political Rights—Parts I, II, and III, or the first 27 Articles (www.ohchr.org/en/professionalinterest/pages/ccpr.aspx).

Instructions: This assignment has two parts. The first involves writing a short paragraph on each of the three types of human rights police social interactions. We ask that you recall a story, or make up a realistic story, that describes your role honoring, or not, human rights for each specific type of interaction. The second part of this assignment asks you to discuss which human rights you find most important to policing today. More specific information for each part of this discussion board follows below.

Part One: Activity

Recall the three types of police social interactions with members of the community as they relate to human rights policing (1) *Assertive Exercise Police Interactions*, (2) *Active Respect Police Interactions*, and (3) *Objective Enjoyment Police Interactions*. Remember that in all of these police interactions with community members, the fulfillment of human rights always depends on the police officer. The community member is always in possession of human rights, whether or not she states (exercises) her rights, remains acutely aware of these rights, or doesn't think about her rights at all. That is, every community member possesses human rights, but does not enjoy (possess the object) their human rights unless the police officer both consciously recognizes and actively respects those rights. As a result, the police officer decides which rights the possessor of human rights enjoys and which rights the police officer will deny them to enjoy. The police officer must remain, at all times, highly aware of all the human rights community members possess, and decide to respect those rights, restrict those rights, or deny and violate those rights to the right-holder.

For this activity, write a story (from your real-life experiences or from a realistic fictional account) that provides the best example of each type of police social interaction with community members. In your story, be sure to be specific in discussing your role as the "duty-bearer" as well as the role of the community member as the "right-holder" throughout the entire interaction. Further, discuss which rights you allowed the community members to enjoy, and which ones you denied them to enjoy, throughout the entire policing interaction. The more detailed, thoughtful, and reflective the better.

Part Two: Activity

What are the most pressing human rights for policing today? Applying human rights goes beyond virtue signaling, or occasionally applying human rights when convenient, or consistently applying one version or understanding of human rights. Rather, applying human rights requires extensive, intended, purposive, hyper-conscious, and highly active thought and action toward one's everyday police work. It requires thinking of new and creative ways to apply human rights to a seemingly endless variety of specific situations. It takes a life-long process of examination, analysis, self-reflection, and self-critique on one's thought and actions while on the job and beyond.

For this activity, write a passage on which human rights (pick three) you find most important to policing, your interpretation of those rights, and why you find them most important to policing. Please select your three human rights from the 30 articles in the United Nations Declaration of Human Rights (see: www.un.org/en/about-us/universal-declaration-of-human-rights) and parts I, II, and III (the first 27 Articles) of the International Covenant on Civil and Political Rights (www.ohchr.org/en/professionalinterest/pages/ccpr.aspx).

In your responses, provide strong examples, powerful stories, and personal experiences to substantiate your points.

Notes

1   Since human rights are inherent in every human, and belong to a human simply because of membership to the *Homo sapiens* species, human rights cannot be taken away regardless of any conditions. People can prevent others from enjoying their human rights, but cannot take away the human rights that belong to them. Any mention of taking away human rights in this book imply taking away people's ability to enjoy human rights that naturally, and permanently, belong to them.

2   Lyrics.com, STANDS4 LLC, 2022. "Love Me, I'm a Liberal Lyrics." Accessed January 8, 2022. www.lyrics.com/lyric/4963530/Phil+Ochs

3   This section draws from chapter five of "A Brief History of Human Rights" of Jack Donnelly's seminal book *Universal Human Rights in Theory and Practice*. See: Donnelly, Jack. *Universal Human Rights in Theory and Practice*, Cornell University Press, 2013). Retrieved from ProQuest Ebook Central, http://ebookcentral.proquest.com/lib/uwlax/detail.action?docID=3138459

4   See: www.un.org/en/about-us/universal-declaration-of-human-rights

5   Again, The United Nations posts The Universal Declaration of Human Rights on their website at www.un.org/en/about-us/universal-declaration-of-human-rights

6   See: www.ohchr.org/EN/ProfessionalInterest/Pages/CCPR.aspx

References

Donnelly, Jack. 2013. *Universal Human Rights in Theory and Practice*. Ithaca: Cornell University Press.

Forbes, Steve, and John Prevas. 2009. *Power Ambition Glory: The Stunning Parallels between Great Leaders of the Ancient World and Today—and the Lessons You Can Learn*. New York: Three Rivers Press.

Lovejoy, Arthur O. 1936. *The Great Chain of Being: A Study of the History of an Idea*. Cambridge, MA: Harvard University Press.

Orwell, George. 2013 (1946). *Politics and the English Language*. London: Penguin Classics.

Thompson, Hunter. 1999. *The Rum Diary: A Novel*. New York: Simon & Schuster Paperbacks.

United Nations. *Universal Declaration of Human Rights*. 1948. www.un.org/en/about-us/universal-declaration-of-human-rights

United Nations (General Assembly). 1966. "International Covenant on Civil and Political Rights." *Treaty Series* 999 (December): 171.

Chapter 3

Police, Power, Agency, and Human Rights

> The love of power is the demon of mankind.
>
> (Friedrich Nietzsche)

Introduction

This chapter analyzes the relationship between power and human rights. We discuss the definition of power and offer a Weberian perspective on the origins of power. In other words, what's power and how do people acquire it? We go on to look at how power can be used in both positive and negative ways, sometimes having far-reaching consequences. Finally, we look at the conditions that explain how those in power can learn to violate the human rights of others, for example moral panics and the creation of folk devils. We also talk about agency versus determinism while stressing how using our potential for human agency makes possible a future for human rights policing. We end with a discussion on what all this has to do with policing.

Quis Custodiet Ipsos Custodes?

> We know that no one ever seizes power with the intention of relinquishing it.
>
> (George Orwell)

> When you feel the desire for power, you should stay in solitude for some time.
>
> (Leo Tolstoy)

"But who will watch the watchmen?" While the early 2nd-century Roman poet and satirist Decimus Junius Juvenal posed this question on the problem with corruptible enforcers enforcing morality (specifically on women), and while moral philosopher Socrates discussed the problem of power corrupting humans toward a path of tyranny, other later social thinkers began to question the problems of authority inherent in any hierarchical system, such as bureaucracy, church, military, police, school, and so on. In 1887, when Archbishop Mandell Creighton of the Church of England objected to the modern tendency to hold (what he perceived as) unnecessarily critical views of authority figures, the English writer and historian Lord John Dalberg wrote a letter to the archbishop in which he penned the now infamous quote "Power tends to corrupt and absolute power corrupts absolutely. Great men are almost always bad men."[1] While some philosophers would argue that people are inherently evil when left to their own devices—Hobbes' *Bellum omnium contra omnes*—others argue that it's not people that are inherently bad but rather it's the power they acquire through their institutional

DOI: 10.4324/9781003220282-4

affiliations. That is, the argument goes, access to power inherently makes people corrupt, or perhaps brings out the evil inherent in human beings.

As late as 2013, the Human Rights Council of the United Nations General Assembly raised the point of *quis custodiet ipsos custodes* and the problem of power and human rights:

> It would be good to report that States and civil society are advancing in the promotion of a culture of democratic thinking, democratic *feeling* and democratic acting. Unfortunately, most areas of human activity seem to be locked into their own logic and dynamic, where democracy is conjured to legitimize the *status quo*, while doing little to give life to the concepts of participation and consultation or to core values of the United Nations, including transparency and accountability. Yet, the spirit of democracy resides in the minds of women and men, and step by step each community, State, and region can claim and reclaim it. This culture of democracy must be home-grown and cannot be exported or imposed top-down. Crucial remains the conviction that the government should serve the people and that its powers must be circumscribed by a Constitution and the rule of law. Juvenal's question *quis custodiet ipsos custodes* (who guards the guardians?) remains a central concern of democracy, since the people must always watch over the constitutional behaviour of the leaders and impeach them if they act in contravention of their duties. Constitutional courts must fulfil this need and civil society should show solidarity with human rights defenders and whistleblowers who, far from being unpatriotic, perform a democratic service to their countries and the world.
>
> (United Nations 2013, 17)

The eternal question of who watches the watchmen, or guards the guardians, "remains a central concern for democracy" and, perhaps more importantly, human rights. The document points out that current forms of "democracy" legitimizes the status quo and fails to adequately protect human rights. While human rights and democratic practices remain core beliefs and values among the people, in almost every way, governments, and other power-wielding institutions, fall well short of delivering true democratic practices that honor human rights. What's more, part of the problem lies in the essence of power itself; power inevitably corrupts. It's up to constitutional courts and demands of civil society to hold people with power accountable, but all too often, the system of checks fails, and often fails miserably. The document even points out that human rights defenders and whistleblowers should not be deemed unpatriotic, but rather people performing their duty to the world exposing the crimes of the powerful. The cases of Edward Snowden, Julian Assange, and Chelsea Manning serve as striking examples.

Edward Snowden, currently living in Russia under asylum, leaked documents to world acclaimed journalist Glenn Greenwald and *The Guardian* exposing the NSA's illegal mass domestic surveillance program of security state officials secretly, illegally, and unconstitutionally spying on millions of innocent people that violated the privacy and human rights of American citizens, among others. The United States Government and much of the mainstream media, both the democrats and republicans, remain largely united to punish this whistleblower for exposing human rights violations under the Espionage Act of 1917.[2] Or look at the cases of Julian Assange and Chelsea Manning, the whistleblowers who exposed the human rights abuses and international war crimes—including the killings of innocent children and journalists—that the United States Government committed. The US Government's prosecution and attempted extradition of Julian Assange for his 2010 WikiLeaks' award-winning publication on the Iraq and Afghanistan war logs and US diplomatic cables showcases how exposing the human rights violations of the powerful can land one in big trouble, regardless of their political affiliation.[1] As the public intellectual, journalist, and former wartime correspondent for the *New York Times* Chris Hedges asserts:

> Your job is to expose the machinations of power, the crimes of power, the lies of power—whoever's in power. And that's precisely what Julian did. When he was going after Bush with the Iraq War Logs, the Democrats loved him. But as soon as his journalistic integrity led him to also expose the inner workings of the Democratic Party establishment, they turned on him as vociferously as the Republicans.
>
> (Hedges 2021)

The British police forced Julian Assange out of London's Ecuadorian Embassy in 2019, and as of this writing, he is being held in a high-security prison in London. The reason, as Glenn Greenwald points out:

> The U.S. and British governments hate Assange because of his revelations that exposed their lies and crimes. … Assange will be locked up for years without any need to prove he is guilty of any crime. He will have been just disappeared: silenced by the very governments whose corruption and crimes he denounced and exposed.
>
> (Greenwald 2020)

In his talk at the People's Forum in New York, Chris Hedges discusses how WikiLeaks cofounder Julian Assange's release of the Iraq War Logs exposed numerous US war crimes that included a "Collateral Murder" video of military personnel gunning down two Reuters journalists and unarmed civilians, routine torture of Iraqi prisoners, cover-ups of thousands of civilian deaths, torture and abuse of hundreds of men and boys, thousands of unreported deaths of Iraqi citizens, and killings of nearly 700 civilians who approached US checkpoints too closely (Hedges 2021).[3] Commenting on how Assange has been hunted down and persecuted for exposing human rights abuses of the powerful, Hedges bluntly states:

> Tyrannies invert the rule of law. They turn the law into an instrument of injustice. They cloak their crimes in a *faux* legality. They use the decorum of the courts and trials, to mask their criminality. Those, such as Julian, who expose that criminality to the public are dangerous, for without the pretext of legitimacy the tyranny loses credibility and has nothing left in its arsenal but fear, coercion and violence.
>
> (Hedges 2021)

Whistleblowers who expose the criminal behavior of the most powerful, including the most wanton of human rights violations, face extreme punishment (Hedges 2021). Hedges points out how the Obama and Biden administrations expanded their drone strike program throughout the Middle East, killing hundreds of innocent civilians in its "global drone war hidden from public view" (Hedges 2021).[4] Air Force intelligence analyst Daniel Hale, who exposed Obama's war crimes and his secret "kill lists," along with eight other whistleblowers, were indicted under the Espionage Act. Of course, these whistleblowers did not hand over secret documents to an enemy combatant, a charge legally necessary to be guilty of espionage, but rather to journal outlets exposing human rights crimes of the powerful.

---

1 See: https://theintercept.com/2020/04/22/watch-the-ongoing-travesty-and-dangers-of-the-prosecution-and-attempted-extradition-of-julian-assange/

In essence, in the United States it is illegal to engage in journalism that exposes the human rights abuses of the powerful. The highest-ranking members of the Biden administration worked in unison with major social media platforms, such as Amazon, to censor thought that goes against established orthodoxy, or views that expose the gaping fractures in hegemony. One can reasonably expect that any challenge to power will be met with aggressive state sanctions. The union of corporate and state power (what many political observers refer to as classic fascism) is made evident when the US government works together with Amazon, and other social media outlets, to monitor and ban information that goes against state-sanctioned orthodoxy (Nelson 2021). The government decides what is "good" or "bad" information and will ban people who express thoughts they deem as "bad" or misinformation from all online platforms with "robust enforcement strategies."[5] The power elite even use times of crisis (i.e., a global pandemic) to normalize the sanction of thoughts and ideas that go against the interests of the powerful. As journalist and public intellectual Glenn Greenwald states:

> If you trust the Biden WH to decree what is "misinformation," these claims have been deemed as such: ★ COVID is transmitted human-to-human (Jan 2020) ★ You should wear masks to protect against COVID (March 2020) ★ It's possible COVID leaked from the Wuhan lab (all of 2020). … If, last March, you encouraged people to wear masks against COVID, the WHO/CDC/Fauci cabal said that was "disinformation." If, throughout 2020, you said it seems possible COVID came from a lab leak, you were banned from social media. Who trusts them to be the Ministry of Truth? … The people who lied repeatedly before the election, saying the authentic Biden documents were "Russian disinformation"—and censored reporting based on that lie—now want to anoint themselves the Ministry of Truth, empowered to censor "disinformation."[6]

Or in the words of independent journalist Caitlin Johnstone:

> They said we need internet censorship because (of) Russians. They said we need internet censorship because (of) Covid. They said we need internet censorship because (of) 1/6.[7] They said we need internet censorship because (of) domestic extremists. Pretty sure they just want internet censorship.[8]

The exposure of the powerful violating human rights often leads to sanctions and censorship, not the enforcement of policies that prevent human rights violations.

It's of little wonder that many people today are beginning to lose trust in their social institutions, including questioning the legitimacy of the political establishment. For example, many people believe that we should all pay our fair share of taxes, yet many people complain about poor people not paying their fair share, despite using social resources themselves. ProPublica recently "obtained a vast trove of Internal Revenue Service data on the tax returns of thousands of the nation's wealthiest people, covering more than 15 years" (Eisinger, Ernsthausen, and Kiel 2021). The report shows how US billionaires pay almost no income tax, and sometimes exactly nothing, despite their massive wealth (this includes income and taxes, stock trades, gambling winnings and even the results of audits). The report states,

> In 2007, Jeff Bezos, then a multibillionaire and now the world's richest man, did not pay a penny in federal income taxes. He achieved the feat again in 2011. In 2018, Tesla founder Elon Musk, the second-richest person in the world, also paid no federal income taxes.
>
> (Ibid)

Warren Buffett paid a 0.1 percent tax rate on income of $125 million between 2014 and 2018 while Jeff Bezos, Elon Musk, and Michael Bloomberg paid less than 3.5 percent as their collective wealth grew beyond one hundred billion. While many hard-working families live paycheck to paycheck, the report concludes,

> Taken together, it demolishes the cornerstone myth of the American tax system: that everyone pays their fair share, and the richest Americans pay the most. The IRS records show that the wealthiest can — perfectly legally — pay income taxes that are only a tiny fraction of the hundreds of millions, if not billions, their fortunes grow each year.
>
> (Ibid)

Consistent with the powerful punishing of whistleblowers for their wrongdoing, how did some of the billionaires respond to the findings of the report? Bloomberg's spokesmen said they would "use all legal means at our disposal to determine which individual or government entity leaked these and ensure that they are held responsible" (Rappeport 2021). On behalf of the extreme rich, the US treasury department argues that "the unauthorized disclosure of confidential government information is illegal," and are referring the matter to the F.B.I. and I.R.S. to make a criminal investigation (Ibid). In other words, the US Biden administration is threatening a criminal investigation on whistleblowers, and perhaps journalists, for exposing the wrongdoings of the most powerful. Even a columnist for the orthodox news outlet the *Washington Post*, Megan McArdle, wonders, "The most exciting thing is … who gave them the information, and how long that person will spend in jail when they're caught."[9] The role of the mass media is to make the power of the ruling political and economic elite appear natural, normal, and inevitable, or put in New Orleans colloquialism, as natural as red beans and rice.

It's clear: challenge those in power, regardless of their wrongdoings and human rights abuses, and the entire weight of their power comes crashing down.[10] Even with all the mechanisms in place to protect human rights—constitutional courts, human rights councils and committees, the constitution and Bill of Rights, human rights organizations, watchdog groups, international human rights organizations, and other more local and regional boards protecting abuses of power—universal human rights serve as a vital concept, but one that remains largely an unfulfilled promise. Or as the human rights scholar Donnelly nicely puts it, "Human Rights Theories and documents point beyond actual conditions of existence to what is possible" (2013, 28). We, as a civilization, remain far from achieving what is possible for human rights.

Perhaps the problem with our failure to fully realize human rights lies with the problem of power itself, or, to remind the reader, as Lord Dalberg puts it, "Power tends to corrupt and absolute power corrupts absolutely." What is it about human beings and their abuse of power once they enter hierarchical institutions? Why do so many humans tend to abuse others, and often violate their human rights, when they achieve any degree of power?

What's clear is that power largely goes unchecked, and when challenged, the powerful use their institutional resources to crush those who expose their crimes and human rights abuses. Greater understanding into the nature of power will illustrate the role of power in society and the dangers of challenging the systems of power.

Defining Power

Power is the ability to coerce people to do what you want, to make them conform to your will, with or without their consent. People use their power when they shape the behavior of others, whether they are aware of it or not, in order to fulfill their own desires. According to the great classical sociologist Max Weber, power is a particular type of social interaction where an individual or group attempts to impose their will on others. Weber states that power, an invisible and abstract concept, can be understood as "the probability that one actor within a social relationship will be in a position to carry out his own will despite resistance, regardless of the basis on which this probability rests" (Weber, Roth, and Wittich 1978). Weber's definition of power in society remains the starting point for many scholars interested in understanding power in society.

The Stanford Prison Experiment provides some evidence into the realities of human nature. On August 14, 1971, in Palo Alto, California, nine college students were "arrested" (fake arrests made to look real with real cops performing the arrest degradation ceremony; the students' neighbors and families bore witness) and taken to the basement of Stanford University and relinquished to student guards.[11] Twenty-four students in total were selected from about 70 who applied for an experiment directed by psychology professor Philip Zimbardo. Out of the 70 students who applied to be a part of the experiment (for $15 per day), nine were assigned as "prisoners" (with three in rotation to fill in later if necessary), and another nine were assigned as "guards." The students were all male and screened to include only those with no criminal record or history of mental illness or drug use.

The prisoners were stripped of their clothing and dressed in prison uniforms. Numbers replaced their names, which the guards used to address the prisoners as an act of disrespect. Guards were given stereotypical "guard" uniforms as well as wooden batons and reflective sunglasses. Guards were told in a private meeting to inflict punishment (though not physical) on prisoners, and to create an "atmosphere of oppression" for the prisoners. By day two, the prisoners had staged a rebellion against the guards; the guards responded accordingly and punished the prisoners. By day four, three of the prisoners had suffered mental and psychological breakdown and were released. Guards withheld food rations, restricted bathroom usage to buckets in their cells, and even put one of the newer replacement prisoners into solitary confinement when he went on a hunger strike due to the conditions. The other prisoners were told he would be released from solitary confinement if the rest of them slept on the floor without a blanket; all but one agreed.

After several observers watched the footage on the cameras and said nothing, recent Ph.D. graduate Christina Maslach came to do interviews and was horrified at the conditions the guards were inflicting on the prisoners. Because of her relationship with Zimbardo and her strong reaction, the experiment was called off after only six days instead of the scheduled two weeks.

The experiment shows how humans abuse power when given power, no matter how minimal that power. Many scholars argue that once most humans gain any degree of power within a hierarchical institution, they tend to abuse their power, often violating the human rights of others. Similar arguments as those used to explain the power abused in the Stanford Prison Experiment also reveal how ordinary people can commit horrific acts, including the torture at Abu Ghraib and the atrocities of the Holocaust, among seemingly endless others.

Abuse of power seems common throughout all time and place in human history. Corporate executives, Wall Street investors, politicians, white-collar professionals, even doctors, lawyers, and judges abuse their power and violate the human rights of people, often, despite their ideological rationalizations and righteous justifications, for their own personal gain, and sometimes simply to exert their power and domination over others.

Within the university, widely thought to be the hallmark of free expression, radical democracy, and egalitarianism, academics sometimes use the institutions of hierarchy to dominate and control colleagues who they may not like for personal reasons. In some cases, once academics acquire even a small degree of power, they abuse that power, using it to punish their colleagues for arbitrary reasons. Even liberal arts professors, many against what they claim to be patriarchal institutions that uphold white privilege, sometimes use these same institutions of hierarchy and domination to exert arbitrary power over their own colleagues, especially against those who express views inconsistent with established orthodoxy. To paraphrase one observer, academic politics is so vicious and bitter because the stakes are so low.[12]

Just like professors are not immune to abuses of power, police are subject to the same tendencies. After all, police, just like those of any other profession, are human, and thereby susceptible to the temptation to commit the same abuses of power and violations of human rights as anyone else. But the question arises, what can we do about it? How can we prevent, for the purposes of this book, police officers abusing their power, something that is seemingly part of human nature? The answer, as will be explained in a later section below, lies in the power of human agency.

The point, power exists everywhere in our society, and in most of our social interactions. Television commercials and mass advertisement serve as propaganda tools that corporations and politicians use to force people into behaviors that they normally would not consider, like buying into the corporate version of the American dream or making them think according to the logic of the corporate imagination.

In the 1920s the tobacco industry had a problem: a social taboo existed against women smoking cigarettes, thereby cutting about 50 percent of their profit. Using the ideas of famous psychologist Sigmund Freud and his nephew Edward Bernays (the father of public relations, i.e., propaganda), the tobacco industry learned how to engineer the consent of the masses through linking people's internal deep, dark, and hidden desires to consumption. In this case, they linked women smoking cigarettes to the feminist movement where women could light their "torches of freedom" to finally declare their independence from men, using slogans like, "You've come a long way baby" advertisements. The propaganda was a huge success as women who smoked increased exponentially.[13]

The tobacco industry took an irrational behavior (giving money to a billionaire industry to get cancer) and made it seem rational (smoking will make me free and independent). Just as corporations began to manipulate people's consumption habits using propaganda (advertisements), the US government learned that they can also use propaganda to influence people to make irrational decisions that benefit the interests of the political elite, like supporting certain wars or gaining political support for politicians. As an example, in his first election campaign, Obama won the Association of National Advertisers' annual advertisement of the year in 2008, beating Apple, Nike, and Coors. Corporations, public relations (propaganda) firms, and advertisement companies advertise, as in sell, presidents and prime ministers, in fact politicians in general, just like Snickers bars, or any other commonly consumed commodity (Sweeney 2009).

As Herman and Chomsky discusses in their seminal book *Manufacturing Consent: The Political Economy of the Mass Media*, the powerful corporate controlled media manufactures the consent of the masses to the wishes of the powerful by controlling the narrative, shaping the debate, and offering solutions within the framework of the status quo (2010). Put differently, the political and economic power elite use the media to manufacture the consent of the masses to support the interests of the powerful. This explains why the media, as explained earlier in the preceding section, imprisons, punishes, or "cancels" journalists who make arguments outside the allowed framework of discourse or who otherwise challenge the ideas and actions of the powerful. In this way, the elite manufactures the consent of the masses to support the interest of the powerful including, among many other things, forever wars, lack of universal healthcare (in the United States, not most of Europe or the Western industrialized world), corporate welfare programs and stimulus packages for the rich (e.g., Cares Act), erosion of the social safety net, privatization, deregulation, elimination of labor unions, and other programs that benefit the richest and most powerful people on the planet. The end of this chapter discusses how the media also manufactures the "enemy" as a scapegoat to deflect blame from the true sources of social problems through media-fabricated moral panics and their folk devils.

Many people argue against welfare programs and free government handouts, and perhaps rightly so, but what few people know, mainly because media controls the narrative and manufactures consent, is that the wealthiest corporations on the planet receive, by far, the greatest welfare benefits—free government handouts of US tax dollars for no work. The United States Government's Cares Act was the largest upward transfer of wealth in human history. This transfer of wealth and power of the super-rich allows big corporations and its billionaires to loot the American treasury (Johnson 2020).

While power is used to transfer wealth and power to the rich, wage genocide, mass incarceration, colonialism, and imperialistic wars, it's also used in more subtle ways, even positive ways, like when we force our children to look both ways before crossing the street. Power is used to advance the interests of corporations and the careers of mid-level employees, like managers who use power to request an employee to complete a task or perform a function. Power dominates the entire economic system and world of work, especially in an economic system that relies on wage work and exploitative wages. Power is used to convince people to go to jobs they do not enjoy (many people go to work mainly out of fear of the consequences of not going, e.g., failing to pay bills, rent, mortgage payments, and so on) to justify their right to existence in a global economic system based on endless profit.

Power can be used for other benevolent reasons. Teachers use power to make students follow rules, parents use it to teach their kids about life, cops use it to prevent people from harming themselves (and others), university professors use it to expose students to new ideas. While power can be used in positive ways, it can also be used for the worst of reasons—fulfill political agendas, increase corporate profit, advance political careers, and serve selfish and self-serving interests. Using power for such desires can lead to disastrous consequences, including the holocaust, mass incarceration, ongoing wars, oppression, violation of human rights, systemic inequality, slavery, and so on. As the highly decorated military general who fought in the Mexican Revolution and WWI Smedley Butler put it in 1935:

> I spent 33 years and four months in active military service and during that period I spent most of my time as a high class muscle man for Big Business, for Wall Street and the bankers. In short, I was a racketeer, a gangster for capitalism. I helped make Mexico and especially Tampico safe for American oil interests in 1914. I helped make Haiti and Cuba a decent place for the National City Bank boys to collect revenues in. I helped in the raping of half a dozen Central American republics for the benefit of Wall Street. I helped purify Nicaragua for the International Banking House of Brown Brothers in 1902–1912. I brought light to the Dominican Republic for the American sugar interests in 1916. I helped make Honduras right for the American fruit companies in 1903. In China in 1927 I helped see to it that Standard Oil went on its way unmolested. Looking back on it, I might have given Al Capone a few hints. The best he could do was to operate his racket in three districts. I operated on three continents. … [to end war] … We must take the profit out of war.
>
> (Butler 2018)

So that's power, but how do people acquire it?

From Where Does Power Derive?

The famous sociologist Max Weber explained three types of authority, or power, in human society (Parsons et al. 1946).

1. *Traditional authority*, passed down through generations, derives from either divine will or natural rights to rule. The biblical quote, "It has been written …," shows how a god inscribes power on tablets that hold permanent legitimacy. The divine right of queens or kings in the medieval ages serves as a good example of traditional authority. Of course, while not the dominant type of authority in modern society, traditional authority still exists in modern families. For example, the parent who, responding to the kid constantly questioning their rules "why do I have to listen to you?" frustratedly replies, "Because I am your father." That's right, traditional authority par excellence. In short, one achieves power through tradition, often the divine right to rule or dominate others based on traditional beliefs and hierarchies.

2. *Rational-Legal Authority* derives from an organization or a ruling regime tied to legal legitimacy and bureaucracy. Power does not derive from a god, nor does it derive necessarily from the attributes of the person in possession of the power. Rather, power derives from one's attachment to an institution. A Catholic priest, whether inspiring or dull, retains the power to administer salvation regardless of a following, due to his attachment to the Catholic Church. The president of the United States, whether a great leader or a tyrant, intelligent or dumb, charming or crass, possesses the power to rule due to her attachment to an institution, not her individual attributes. The same goes for professors. Students listen to a professor's lectures even if the professor tires and bores students, emits sounds of auditory terrorism, rambles idiotically, or inspires the intellect. Professors derive power from an institution that granted them title: Doctor of Philosophy and university professor. Police have the power to arrest and, perhaps, even command respect, not due to their potentially wonderful individual qualities, but rather due to their institutional affiliation with a legitimate law enforcement organization. That is, without the badge, the ability of police to arrest, give tickets, and require others to respect the law would become impotent. Police power, like most power today, derives completely from institutional attachment. Put differently, without the institution most people have no power.

3. *Charismatic Authority* derives from a person's ability to impart the belief to others that one has supernatural or superhuman qualities. The charismatic leader can break the hard bonds of tradition or the all-too-frequent irrationality of cold and indifferent rational-legal bureaucracy. As the biblical quote goes, "It has been written … but now I say unto you…" perhaps best exemplifies the power of charisma. Of course, charisma can produce mixed results—from Hitler's Nazi Germany to war mongers like Hillary Clinton and George Bush, to peaceful protesters like Gandhi and Martin Luther King.

It's important to understand the relationship between authority and trust. Authority relies on at least some degree of trust. Even when queens and kings failed to deliver on their divine obligations to the people, there were often organized bodies to dispose of their rulership. Even in the most absolutist type of authoritative regimes, trust bears some role. Just as power derives from institutional affiliation, so does trust. For example, at the beginning of every semester, my students, to whom I am a stranger, do not have trust in me as an individual, or a unique person. After all, I'm but a stranger to their world. Rather, they trust the institution that I represent. Put differently, they trust me only *through* the institution. That is, people will trust you as well as they trust the institution that gives you power—the institution of law enforcement. Loss of trust in the institution translates to loss of trust in you, regardless of how wonderful or awful your police work. Put differently, just as your power derives from your institutional affiliation, so does the trust that the public has in you. This is true of any profession. A Catholic priest loses heart when the flock loses faith in the church. I remember one student who told me that she never listened to the views of her professors. After all, as her parents said, universities serve as institutional tools for communists to spread their leftist, Marxist, ideology on the vulnerable. When the Catholic Church or university loses its legitimacy, or trust, in the eyes of the public, the public loses trust in the people tied to those institutions (priest, professor, cop) regardless of how good they are at their jobs. Yes, it's unfair for the individual, but nonetheless a hard fact. In short, the loss of faith in law enforcement is not personal, and has little to do with most individual police officers. Rather, it has to do with the institution to which police officers are a part, even if they, as individuals, unfairly bear the brunt of the critique.

We can't control what happened regarding the public's trust in the institution of law enforcement, but we can control our response to the public's response. Of course, we believe human rights policing serves as the best response, and the path forward for the profession of law enforcement to reclaim its trust with the public fostering a healthy, trusting relationship to police and those they protect and serve. But what are the first steps to realizing human rights policing? How do you, specifically as a police officer, make the first steps to applying human rights policing? The first chapters provided you with the intellectual framework to understand human rights and your responsibility as police officers to ensure the protection of the human rights of all people. Now we turn to the concept of charisma and realizing your ability to use the power of human agency to become even better at your jobs, to become the best law enforcement agents and police officers known to the world.

Weber's notion of charisma served as a rather optimistic viewpoint to understand social change. If humans wish to break free from the shackles of traditional authority, or cold sterile rational-legal authority that traps people in an iron cage, the hope lies in a charismatic figure to disrupt such authority types to usher in a new course in history. While Weber's notion of the charismatic figure, or Nietzsche's concept of the *Übermensch* (superhuman), relies largely on a single charismatic figure, we believe in the power of the individual to become charismatic—a positive force for change in this world. Specifically, we believe that police officers, as individuals, can become charismatic figures to make change and bring about human rights policing to their departments. Police officers and law enforcement agents must ask themselves what they want to do with the power they possess. It's a question they must first ask in their own hearts. In short, what do you want to do with the power derived from institutional affiliation?

Everyone can become their own type of charismatic leader to make positive changes in the world while still operating within their institutions. Charisma requires both realizing and employing human agency, in your everyday life and careers.

Quis custodiet ipsos custodes? Perhaps it's your sense of agency as law enforcement professionals to protect the human rights and dignity of all humans while dealing with the many challenges you face in both your life and career.

But first, you must learn to use the power of human agency, to which we now turn.

Human Agency Versus Determinism

Human agency, though somewhat similar, differs from the theological concept of free will. Free will, or the ability for the individual to make choices without any interfering internal or external factors, remains a point of contention in the world of theology. This contention lies with the theological fatalism, the paradox of free will, that shows the contradiction between an omnipotent god and free will. In theological determinism, the doctrine of predestination holds the view that "everything which happens has been predestined to happen by an omniscient, omnipotent divinity" (Iannone 2001, 148). Therefore, if God knows and determines everything in a predestined world, the idea of free will becomes problematic.

Similarly, the problem between free will and determinism also arises in philosophy. As Bertrand Russell states, "The contradiction between free will and determinism is one of those that run through philosophy from early times to our own day, taking different forms at different times" (Russell 1945, 266). For the stoic philosophers, "cosmic determinism and human freedom" remained a central concern with the belief that "there is no such thing as chance, and that the course of nature is rigidly determined by natural laws" (Russell 1945, 254). Here philosophy, as in theology, must deal with the fundamental contradiction that, "On the one hand, the universe is a rigidly deterministic single whole, in which all that happens is the result of previous causes. On the other hand, the individual will is completely autonomous" (Russell 1945, 266). Put as a question, how can an individual be completely autonomous with her full individual free will while simultaneously existing in a universe, or cosmos, that is a rigidly deterministic single whole? The contradiction finds an uneasy remedy with the idea that the universe, or God, is completely free, and the individual, part of the universe as any other material and non-material element, carries out the will of the universe. That is, the individual is determined to carry out the free will of the universe.

Human nature also presents another problem with the ideas of individual free will for the human animal. The ancient Greek philosopher Epicurus (341–270 BC) argued that people are always in constant pursuit of their own desire for pleasure. That is, the primary innate drive of the human being is to pursue pleasure and avoid pain. This desire for pleasure and fear of pain drives all men "who at all times, pursue only their own pleasure, sometimes wisely, sometimes unwisely" (Russell 1945, 245). Other philosophers like Jeremy Bentham and John Locke also held general theories on humankind that all people are determined to "always be moved, in action, solely by desire for his own happiness or pleasure" (Russell 1945, 613). If we are always in constant pursuit of pleasure and avoidance of pain, how can free will exist?

The famous psychologist Sigmund Freud believes that not much distinguishes human animals from non-human animals. He argues that human beings, far from striving toward perfection or higher moral and ethical goals, strive to fulfill their own selfish pursuit of pleasure and avoidance of pain. He argues that any belief otherwise serves as a perfectly convenient illusion, one that gives pleasure to believe. Freud says:

> Many of us will also find it hard to abandon our belief that in man himself there dwells an impulse towards perfection, which has brought him to his present heights of intellectual prowess and ethical sublimation, and from which it might be expected that his development into superman will be ensured. But I do not believe in the existence of such an inner impulse, and I see no way of preserving this pleasing illusion. The development of man up to now does not seem to me to need any explanation differing from that of animal development, and the restless striving towards further perfection which may be observed in a minority of human beings is easily explicable as the result of that repression of instinct upon which what is most valuable in human culture is built.
>
> (1922)

That instinct, in Freudian psychoanalysis, is the pleasure principle which asserts humankind's instinctual drive to pursue pleasure and avoid pain to satisfy psychological and biological needs. In that way, the same deterministic instinctual drives that determine the behavior of non-human animals also determine the behavior of human animals.

Perhaps anthropologists and sociologists serve as the last of the world's romantics, at least some of us. While the idea of free will is an anthropological impossibility in the world of the social sciences, the concept of human agency emerges as a response to the free will and determinism debate.

Agency, in our view, is the most beautiful word in the English language. Agency is the ability to carve your own will in a world that attempts to deny it. Agency makes change possible and offers hope in a world in dire need of it. Without agency, simply put, human civilization will continue its suicidal path of war, death, violence, suffering, and self-destruction. Human agency makes it possible to avoid such a fate.

Agency is the ability for human beings to go against the grain of determinism. That is, human agency is the ability for the individual to make thoughts and decisions that go against their biological instincts (inner unruly forces) and social conditioning (external drives). Simply put, agency, if it exists, is truly an extraordinary concept.

But how can one go against determinism?

Many philosophers and social scientists believe this to be impossible. Human beings, many believe, are as determined as any other animal. Certainly, throughout all of human history, people seem to follow their instincts of socialization, group belonging, and creating outside enemies that strengthen the solidarity of the group. Humans have sex and reproduce because it feels good (birthrates would probably drop if such experiences brought pain), obediently consume because it feels good, and get old and die because of biological fate. This behavior does not appear entirely different from other animals. To quote Freud's observation again, "The development of man up to now does not seem to me to need any explanation differing from that of animal development" (Freud 1922). But Freud was no romantic.

We are romantics. We believe in the power of human agency. We believe that human beings have the ability to go against the grain of their biological instincts and socialized conditioning.[14]

That is, we believe that human agency can overcome human nature and determinism. Again, it's an extraordinary concept, quite romantic, and in the truest sense of the word, an awesome ability.

But there's a catch.

We might possess the *potential* for human agency, but most of us never *realize* it. Of course, we might think we use it, because the alternative is rather difficult to accept. Most people simply do as they are told—enact their socially prescribed script, fulfill their societal roles, and conform to the logic of the system. Most people are rather ordinary, automated, mechanistic, and determined. Our political and economic system subdues most people to basic formulae, crushes individuality, withers imagination, destroys spontaneity, cripples intellect, negates the soul, domesticates the spirit, "rubricates" education, slows comprehension, demands conformity, and expects obedience. The cold, hard truth is that most people never use their potential for agency, which, in essence, makes them existentially dead. Most people simply sleepwalk through their waking life.

But when we use our agency, we go above and beyond societal expectations, we rise above the ordinary, we realize our self and fulfill our potentialities. When we use our agency, and only when we use our agency, are we really alive. Only then do we arise from our existential slumber to become alive, aware, fully conscious, self-actualizing, self-transcendent beings capable of free thought and action. Failing to use agency results in existential death, to become part of the "sheeple" herded along to our waiting graves. We ask police officers and criminal justice professionals to become fully aware of how internal drives and external forces determine human behavior, and further, to appreciate how rare it is to use the power of our agency among the human species. Only then can you ever begin the potential to realize your agency, think freely, liberate your heart, realize your full potential, indeed essence, to become full original and free human beings.

The success of human rights policing largely relies on criminal justice professionals and law enforcement agents to realize their own essence, or sense of agency, to realize their full potential as human beings, to become everything they were intended to become, to go beyond the ordinary, and to rise beyond the limited expectations imposed upon them.

In short, the realization of human rights policing largely depends on the ability of police officers and law enforcement agents to not only understand their potential for agency, but to realize their agency in all of their interactions with members of the community while conducting police work. What's more, outside of police work and the criminal justice system, realizing our potential for agency as human beings makes our life more meaningful.

Police officers and criminal justice professionals realizing their potential for human agency to implement human rights in their police work will not only change how the community (national and local) views law enforcement, but will actually improve their ability to protect and serve humanity. When public trust in policing improves, trust in police officers improves. Perhaps it's time for police officers and criminal justice professionals to use their agency to impart their subjective imprint onto the institution of law enforcement and criminal justice. Perhaps police officers would be wise to remind themselves why they became cops and imagine imparting *themselves* into the institution of policing. That is, don't let the culture of policing change you, instead, change the culture of policing. For police officers it's important to ask "how did I use my human agency today?" to remain fully aware of the potential for human agency in order to realize it in all of their encounters with people while protecting and serving the community.

Here's a story inside the New Orleans Police Department that applies human agency to police work.

Human Agency and Policing: A Story from Inside the N.O.P.D.

The tensions between human agency and determinism have powerful implications on human behavior. It's amazing to see, and recognize agency. That was certainly the case at one time in my career, especially during a long assignment to the Narcotics Unit. It took me a while to recognize it, but there was one man in that unit who exercised his agency more than any other detective.

It all started when my partner and I went through a transformation. I had just got assigned to the unit along with my old partner. We had both being assigned to the Special Operation Unit. Apparently, we had been leading the numbers game in the area of narcotics enforcement when the powers that be in the department noticed our achievements and asked us to transfer to the Narcotics Unit.

At first, I was not so interested since I was happy in my old unit. I reluctantly accepted, and decided it was my fate after learning that we were being assigned a brand-new car, money to buy dope, access to all the equipment we needed, and weekends off. When we arrived at our new assignment, we found that there was an ongoing transformation. While some of the old personnel was transferring out, we were being moved from Headquarters to a non-descript building in a residential neighborhood. New rank in charge was also in charge of the two platoons. Interestingly, my new sergeant shared the same rank of patrol officer as me. He was just given command of the platoon based on his knowledge of the narcotics business and time in the unit. Adding to his new position was the fact that the Department and Civil Service had not promoted sergeants and lieutenants for some time as it waited on the outcome of some litigation.

When I began to work, I noticed that there was something different about our new leader. He was changing things around. Put differently, he was using his agency to make the unit better. He immediately set about changing the police reports the unit had been writing. We were now taught and required to include much more detail. For example, during a surveillance of a house reported to be selling cocaine, we sent an informant with our money to make a small purchase as part of the basis for a search warrant. I was actually in a van in front of the house and could observe the front door when the informant knocked on the door, was greeted, and made the purchase. When the warrant was served and cocaine was found, several arrests were made. I was in charge of writing the report. Our new supervisor, whom I will call James, came to me and asked me what I had seen during my surveillance. After I told him that I had seen our informant purchase what turned out to be cocaine, he asked what hand he used to exchange the money. I asked to myself, "What hand did he use to receive the package?" Having observed the transaction so closely, I recalled what hands were used. Those and many other details were now to be incorporated into our reports.

This was a new day in the Narcotics Unit.

After that change, and many others, our conviction rate rose and the unit forged a new reputation in the Department and District Attorney's Office.

But the most impressive demonstration of agency was yet come.

It was the time we had been working on a case involving the distribution of cocaine. I was working undercover buying several kilos of cocaine at the targets house. An informant introduced me to a man and his organization selling coke. Finally, the time came for me to order a large amount of cocaine and hit the target with arrests and search warrants. By now, we had become very proficient in the execution of no-knock warrants. We were to execute the protocol for high-risk warrants since I had often seen our target carrying a gun on his side while dealing with me at his house.

As per protocol, we parked our vehicles some distance away to be very quiet and use the element of surprise. Two officers would carry the ram, knock down the door, drop it, and stand back while the rest of us wearing bullet proof jackets and shotguns, entered the house screaming, "Police with a search warrant!"

The plan called for us to spread throughout the house looking for people and dope. I was the third officer in the line to enter, and James, our acting sergeant, was the first through the door.

As I entered, I saw our target, the man who was always carrying a gun and who masterminded a cocaine organization, pointing a large pistol at James. James had his shotgun aimed at the target in a standoff. Both men were staring at each other for what looked like an eternity. I was about to turn my full attention and shotgun toward this man when I saw him throw his gun at the feet of James telling him, "I give up."

In the quick pace of the event, I kept going through the house and found several other people, also armed, and several kilos of cocaine. The operation was successful as we disrupted a major cocaine organization and seized a large amount of cocaine.

But the standoff stayed in my mind to the point where I could not sleep that night. The next day, as I entered the office, I went straight to James' office and asked in my first sentence to him, "Why didn't you shoot that man?" James looked at me for a moment saying nothing. I repeated, "Why didn't you shoot him?" Finally, he replied, "I looked at the man's eyes and I saw calm, I could tell that he was not going to shoot me. I didn't see death in his eyes."

Talk about agency.

Police culture, a form of determinism, would have had James shoot in that confrontation. However, we already knew that James used his agency for change. It was his use of agency that allowed James to hold that trigger and evaluate the situation. He used his agency to transform a unit and save a life. That's a fine example of human rights policing.

Police Officer David Pehl of the University of Wisconsin La Crosse Police Department

A university campus police officer offers another example on how employing one's human agency, even in small acts, makes a big difference in the lives of police officers and those they serve.

> I have seen many changes in law enforcement during my twenty-seven years of service. While the tactics, training, and way of doing things have changed to meet the needs and times, one of the biggest changes involves my personal philosophy of policing. Success in law enforcement requires an officer to accept change and remain flexible. Not only in policing tactics but also in one's thinking and mind set. For example, I went from a newly minted rookie who saw the world in black and white and right or wrong to a veteran who now sees the world as a little black, a little white, and a whole lot gray. Remaining flexible and using discretion to do my job serves as the greatest benefit to me. As I look back, there were times when I didn't know anything other than black or white and right or wrong. My job was harder because I had not yet learned flexibility. I will admit that sometimes I responded the wrong way or made the wrong decision. I sometimes made those situations worse because I didn't have that wisdom and flexibility that you get from years of experiences and development.
>
> When I learned flexibility, something remarkable happened. I realized my actions had meaning. I started to think differently and to see things from different perspectives. I started to look at the "why something happened," along with the "what happened." Rarely does something happen without reason.
>
> I'm specifically thinking about a traffic stop that occurred about ten years ago. I was on a patrol as a car passed me in the opposite direction. I saw a child in the back that without a child seat. I pulled over the vehicle and found a three-year-old child sitting in the back without a safety seat. In talking to the mom, I found out that she had recently lost her job and was struggling to make ends meet. She was making difficult decisions and sacrifices. She couldn't afford a child seat since her money was being spent of food and shelter with very little left over. The rookie in me would have given her a ticket and called someone to safely transport the child.
>
> That would have started a series of events that would cause more harm than good. She would have chosen food and shelter instead of paying her ticket. Her license would have been suspended and a warrant would be issued. The next time she was pulled over for not having a child in a seat, she would be arrested and go to jail as her child would have to go with child protective services and her car probably towed. This could have easily caused a lot of "unseen" harm. As examples of unseen harm, the arrested mother may experience the shame of being arrested in front of her child, law enforcement would be seen as an adversary, and a child might be traumatized as the result of being taken their mom and placed in emergency foster care. Further, the mother might lose her only means of transportation. The spiral of unseen harm would continue with the mothing possibly losing her job as the result of her car being towed. Of course, getting fired translates no more money. Without money, she may be evicted from her house and left and be homeless on the hard streets. One wonders, is all of this worth the cost for having a child improperly seated in a car. Now don't get me wrong, car seats protect children and it's something that

needs to be corrected. A better way is to start looking at human situations from a human rights perspective and see what we can do to help someone, rather than harm them.

When talking with the mother, she told me that she carried guilt and shame because she didn't have her child restrained properly. Having grown up in poverty, I could relate to the struggles that she was having. As a parent of a child around the same age, I also could see the love that she holds for her child.

By looking at the "why" rather than the "what," I realized a solution that was beneficial to her and her child yet still enforced the law. I told her to remain at the scene while I went back to my police department. I took a car seat out of my own vehicle as I had a child around the same age and brought it back to the scene. I installed it properly and ensured that her daughter was securely and properly restrained. The little girl was thrilled at the pink color. The relief on the mother's face told me that I had made the right decision. Although it was a small gesture, it had an immense effect. The guilt and shame that she felt for putting her child in that situation instantly washed away. As police officers not only should we be on the lookout for crime and people causing problems, but we should also be looking for ways that we can be that one person who took the time to care for a fellow human being.

By that simple act of compassion, the situation had a completely different outcome that will reverberate into the future. I looked at her as a struggling mother who needed a little help rather than a law breaker. We need to look at people in situations as humans rather than people that are drug addicts, homeless, or law breakers. Look at the why they are in those positions and how they got there rather than just looking at the current moment. They are more than their addiction or homelessness or their momentary situation.

When people talk about important traits to have for law enforcement officers, I believe courage, integrity, and honor are among the top qualities. One trait that I think is missing on this list is compassion.

Threats to Human Rights Policing: Moral Panics and the Manufacturing of Folk Devils

Crime exists in every society, not because crime is "real" or a matter of truth or objective fact, but rather because a society constructs certain acts as deviant, thereby manufacturing the outsider, and sometimes, the criminal. The classical sociologists Emile Durkheim says it best:

> Imagine a society of saints, a perfect cloister of exemplary individuals. Crimes, properly so called, will there be unknown; but faults which appear venial to the layman will create there the same scandal that the ordinary offense does in ordinary consciousness. If, then, this society has the power to judge and punish, it will define these acts as criminal and will treat them as such.
>
> (Durkheim 1958)

In other words, even in a society of saints, there will be sinners. Durkheim argues that crime is normal and inevitable in society, in fact, socially determined, because it serves a useful social function—the creation of "criminal" outsiders strengthens the social solidarity of the inside group. In other words, if a community is to remain together, it must create an evil, outside group to strengthen its internal solidarity and collective consciousness. Crime functions to strengthen the solidarity of the group, state, country, and/or society (Hawdon, Ryan, and Agnich 2010).

The Chicago School former jazz musician turned sociologist Howard Becker argues that society creates the criminal, not due to social conditions creating crime or necessarily "bad" people violating laws, but rather:

> Social groups create deviance by making the rules whose infraction constitutes deviance, and by applying those rules to particular people and labeling them as outsiders. From this point of view, deviance is not a quality of the act the person commits, but rather a consequence of the application by others of rules and sanctions to an "offender." The deviant is one to whom that label has successfully been applied; deviant behavior is behavior that people so label.

> (Becker 1963, 1–18)

Deviance is not a quality inherent in an act, but rather a quality other, usually more powerful, people bestow upon an act. For example, killing another human with a gun is either deviant or heroic depending on how the act is interpreted within a given situation.

This is not to say people don't commit awful acts of violence or deny that rotten people exist. Of course they do. But who becomes labeled as rotten and awful becomes an important question for analysis. Wealthy men and women with business suits are not often thought of as criminals, thugs, killers, and thieves. In fact, they mostly go unpoliced in society and unexamined in the halls of academia. In their book *The Rich Get Richer, The Poor Get Prison*, Criminologists Jeffrey Reiman and Paul Leighton argue that the rich commit society's most destructive crimes related to financial damage and loss of human life, but the criminal justice system is directed almost entirely toward the poorest Americans whose crimes inflict the least damage in society (Reiman and Leighton 2020). This is quite interesting when crimes of the powerful account for about 90 percent of all killings and financial loss in society. Put positively, police officers and criminologists devote almost all of their attention to only 10 percent of all crime: street crime. Put negatively, police officers and criminologists ignore most of the crime that causes the greatest harm in society.

According to legend, bank robber Pretty Boy Floyd destroyed mortgage notes when he robbed banks to ensure that banks could not foreclose on poor families suffering through the Great Depression and Dust Bowl.[15] Floyd was killed in 1934, during the height of the Great Depression, an era many commentators compare with present day conditions of massive tax cuts for the rich, strengthening the welfare state for the rich, and depleting resources for working Americans. Woody Guthrie's song, "Pretty Boy Floyd" (1939) captures the essence of crime and the criminal in the brief excerpt below:

> Yes, as through this world I've wandered
> I've seen lots of funny men
> Some will rob you with a six-gun
> And some with a fountain pen.[16]

In other words, while most people assume the poor are most likely to commit crime, there is little reason to doubt that the poor and rich are just as likely to commit crime. If a poor man decides to become a criminal, he will use whatever resources he needs to commit the crime, such as a knife or gun. On the other hand, if a rich woman decides to become a criminal, she will use the resources at her disposal to commit the crime—access to state and corporate resources, the finance industry, and technology. Or as Guthrie pointed out, some rob you with a gun while others rob you with a pen. The only difference is that crimes of the powerful, done with resources like fountain pens, cause far more violence and financial loss than all the street crime combined. This difference begs the questions: why do we focus our police work almost solely on street crime? Why do we fear street crime the most when political and corporate crime is a far bigger threat to our lives and financial security? Why do we fear the "street thug" over the far more dangerous corporate or political thug? And for the purposes of this book, why are we far more likely to violate the rights of working-class and poor people than the elites who are just as likely to commit crime?

Every society manufactures its own folk devils serving to dehumanize people turned evil outsiders. The process of creating folk devils happens through the engineering of moral panics.

Moral panics are manufactured societal fears, exaggerated accounts of some deviant groups that threaten to destroy society. Moral entrepreneurs, official "authorities" (mental health experts, social scientists, "experts," social workers, councilors, religious organizations, private interest groups), and mass (and social) media create these often-exaggerated stories, or narratives, about some deviant behavior intended to generate sudden and widespread terror or fear among the mainstream public. Moral panics often result in collective responses of concern and hostility toward a newly perceived threat from social pariahs and "folk devils" deemed evil (Cohen 2011; Goode and Nachman Ben-Yehuda 1994).

Moral panics display five main characteristics that involve (1) concern that the deviant group's behavior is a real threat capable of causing societal and personal harm, (2) hostility toward the perceived deviant group that develops into a clear division between "us" and "them," where the deviant group becomes full-fledged folk devils, (3) consensus among enough members of the general public that the threat to society is real, setting up the emergence of moral entrepreneurs to become vocal against a perceived weaker and disorganized folk-devil group, (4) disproportionality of the actions or planned actions taken against the perceived threats of the deviant group, and (5) volatility, where panics disappear almost as suddenly as they arise due to newly emerging public interests that often develop in the mass media (Ibid).

Moral panics remain a large part of contemporary society and the culture of fear ever present in our "if you see something, say something" culture. This strong and widespread fear captures, at least temporarily, the attention of the public, convincing them that the evil is real and may very well come knocking on your waiting door.

The folk devil is the boogieman, a social type that reminds us all of what we must never become: the "personification of evil." This is the stuff of Britain's 1950s mods and rockers and 1960s Teddy Boys, London's and New York's punks (Sex Pistols and Dead Boys, respectively; working-class youth from London's East End, Hip-Hop inner-city youths, and Afro-European Rastas)—"out of control" youth subcultures of resistance. Moral panics and their folk devils include Hillary Clinton's urban black "superpredator," Nixon's black civil rights activists and leftist war protesters in his manufactured and still ongoing war on drugs, Wilson's first and McCarthy's second red scare against anarchists and communists, Roosevelt's internment camps of Japanese Americans, and so on. Today we have no shortage of moral panics and their folk devils—many that are indeed deemed evil. We have a culture of fear with a whole slew of devils that include Black Lives Matter activists, anarchists and looters, illegal immigrants and refugees, heroin and meth users, youth gangs, inner-city youths wearing hoodies and sagging pants, Islamic terrorists and their sympathizers, street thugs and school shooters, drunken drivers and hate criminals, Marxists and radicals, a youth gone wild and urban "savages" roaming nighttime streets, among dozens of others.

The power elite (generally referring to those that control our political and economic institutions) have always used moral panics as a powerful tool to manipulate people into doing things they would normally not even consider—the essence of power. Creating moral panics and folk devils is nothing new, rather, it's a long-used trope throughout history. Powerful groups use moral panics to incite fear and anger among a population using the media and education, among other institutions, to manipulate and control the masses. It's an incredibly effective tool—manufacturing folk devils creates the illusion of "outsiders" against a good group of "insiders" morally opposed to the "evil other" who becomes scapegoated for societal problems (poverty, crime, unemployment, lower standard of living, epidemics, war, disease, and so on). Creating folk devils through moral panics that "threaten to destroy" society is an age-old trick used to manipulate the masses often leading to authoritarian control of the population, high incarceration rates, punitive criminal justice policies, and wars (domestic and international), among other things.

In short, creating the folk devil is a way to dehumanize people. It's more difficult to kill, murder, lynch, abuse, torture, deport, and terrorize people without first taking away their humanity. In short, moral panics create folk devils that strip people of their humanity.

This process of creating the folk devil runs throughout American history, including people deemed "non-white" by the dominant culture, like the "swarthy" Germans during their early immigration to the United States. Or in the words of the highly revered Benjamin Franklin:

> Which leads me to add one Remark: That the Number of purely white People in the World is proportionably very small. All Africa is black or tawny. Asia chiefly tawny. America (exclusive of the new Comers) wholly so. And in Europe, the Spaniards, Italians, French, Russians and Swedes, are generally of what we call a swarthy Complexion; as are the Germans also, the Saxons only excepted, who with the English, make the principal Body of White People on the Face of the Earth. I could wish their Numbers were increased.[17]

The Germans, Irish, Italians, Hungarians, Russians, Jews, and so on were largely considered a "swarthy" people, and in turn, at one moment of history, each group was dehumanized using moral panics. For example, the mainstream American media commonly depicted the Irish as "Celtic ape-men with sloping foreheads and monstrous appearances" and "menacing names like the Black Snakes and Rough and Readies" that were criminals and rapists. "No Irish Need Apply" signs were plastered all over the place as it was believed that such an ape-like creature could never assimilate into white, decent, American society. Just about every immigrant group received similar experiences in the United States through moral panics and a process of dehumanization. This dehumanization process justified seemingly countless acts of violence and violations of human rights.[18] In short, we, as a human species, can justify violating human rights, or worse, after we dehumanize a group of people.[19] Once people become perceived as less than human (animals, thugs, criminals, "bad hombres," super-predators, Celtic ape-men, and so on) it becomes possible to commit acts of violence against them, violate their human rights, and take away their dignity. Powerful groups have always used moral panics to dehumanize people, and it always allows us to mistreat our fellow humans.

Moral panics and the manufacturing of folk devils threatens human rights policing, just as they threaten the safety and security of the people. Human rights policing depends on maintaining the human rights of all people regardless of their dehumanized perceptions in the popular imagination. In other words, human rights policing requires us to refuse to believe that any individual or group of people are folk devils. Rather, just like you and me, they have human agency, hopes for the future, meaningful experiences, romantic feelings, fear of pain and suffering, and personal honor and dignity. The media and politicians create social pariahs, but, as law enforcement agents and police officers, we refuse to accept such perceptions of people, treat each individual based on their own character, and honor their human rights, even when most difficult.

Alas, we have agency.

This chapter ends with a brief story and a question.

Black Mirror: "Men Against Fire"

An episode titled "Men Against Fire" in the British program *Black Mirror* showcases a perfect metaphorical example of how certain groups of people become dehumanized, especially in cases of war. The main protagonist, Stripe, is a young military soldier in combat against an enemy. He is partnered with an ambitious soldier, fittingly named Hunter, who enjoys hunting the enemy. Although the soldiers have American accents, it remains unclear which military they serve. Stripe has been well trained to shoot and kill humanoid bug-like figures called Roaches. And the Roaches are despised. They are the personification of evil, evil par excellence. All the viewer knows in the beginning is that the Roaches are the enemy and the military takes pride in finding and shooting them. Soon, however, Stripe begins having trouble with his vision. He starts to see the Roaches as humans begging for their lives. It appears to be some sort of technical difficulty with his vision, and we come to find out that all soldiers have been implanted with something called MASS that changes the way they see the enemy. It turns out that the Roaches are in fact humans, and that the MASS devices allow the soldiers to see them as alien-like creatures in order to make killing them easier. The military psychiatrist who treats Stripe after his MASS glitches reveals that while soldiers in the past had trouble shooting the enemy directly, MASS allows them to do so with ease and without any trauma, and soldiers are rewarded with pleasant dreams if they kill Roaches.

This backfires when the glitch in Stripe's MASS continues, and he saves a woman and her son from being killed by Hunter as he sees them as humans instead of Roaches. Upon escaping with the woman and her son, she reveals that her people are victims of ethnic cleansing and genocide by the military. In the end, Hunter finds Stripe and the Roaches in hiding, kills them and knocks Stripe out. Stripe awakens in the psychiatrist's facility where it is revealed that Stripe consented to the MASS device before signing up for the military. Stripe is faced with the choice of being imprisoned for trying to save the enemy or having his memory wiped and his MASS reset. He chooses the latter.

Obviously, we don't have MASS devices preventing us from seeing reality. On the other hand, the mass media shapes our reality in powerful ways that we cannot fully see. And just like Stripe, you have a choice. What do you see, and further, how will you, as a police officer or criminal justice professional treat the individual, as a folk devil, or as a human being deserving of their rights?

Suggested Activities

Activity One: Applying your Human Agency to Police Work

Recall from the chapter that agency is the ability of human beings to go against the grain of determinism. That is, human agency is the ability of the individual to make thoughts and decisions that go against their biological instincts (unruly inner forces) and social conditioning (external drives). In short, human agency, if it exists, allows us the potential to overcome human nature and determinism. It's an extraordinary concept, but there's a catch.

We might possess the *potential* for human agency, but most of us *never* realize it. We might think we do, but we often confuse agency with the ability to make decisions. But agency goes far beyond the simple ability to make decisions; rather, it allows us to go against the internal and external forces driving our behavior. When we use our agency, we go above and beyond societal expectations, we rise above the ordinary, we realize ourselves and fulfill our potentialities.

The success of a human rights policing largely relies on you, as law enforcement agents, using your own essence, or sense of agency, to realize your full potential as human beings, to become everything you were intended to become, to go beyond the ordinary, and rise beyond the limited expectations imposed upon you. In short, the realization of human rights policing largely depends on your ability as police officers and law enforcement agents to not only understand your potential for agency, but to realize your agency in all of your interactions with members of the community while conducting police work.

Provide two or three stories from your policing experiences where you realized (or not) your potential for human agency while conducting police work or interacting with members of the community. Please use specific examples or stories from your work experiences. If you realized your potential for human agency, what happened? How did it impact your interaction with community members or impact your potentials as a police officer? If you recall a situation where you did not use your human agency, but in retrospect wish you did, how could you have used your human agency in the encounter? What do you think the results may have been? Explain.

Two: Do We Possesses the Potential for Human Agency?

Do you believe that people possess the potential for human agency? Do you believe people ever realize this potential in their actions? Please provide a story from your personal experiences (on or off the job) that gives evidence to your answers. Do you have human agency? Explain.

Three: Can Applying Human Agency Improve Human Rights Policing?

How might police officers realizing their potential for using their human agency while conducting police work and interacting with members of the community serve, perhaps even improve, the law enforcement profession? Do you believe that police officers applying their human agency in police work can help achieve the goals for human rights policing? Either way, please explain.

Four: Policing and Folk Devils

While we don't have MASS devices preventing us from seeing reality, the mass media shapes our reality in powerful ways that we cannot fully see. Given that the creation of moral panics and folk devils heavily influence public perceptions of specific groups of people throughout history, do you think it also impacts how police officers and law enforcement agents view these same groups? In other words, do you think that the creation of folk devils through moral panics, and other such media tactics, impacts how police officers view some of the people they police? Do you think it impacts how police officers treat people differently based on those perceptions? If so, at least for some, what suggestions would you offer to other police officers about treating other groups negatively portrayed in the media?

Notes

1 Historical essays & studies by John Emerich Edward Dalberg-Acton, first baron Acton; edited by John Figgis and Reginald Vere Laurence. See: https://oll.libertyfund.org/title/laurence-historical-essays-and-studies

2 See: Glenn Greenwald at https://theintercept.com/2020/04/22/watch-the-ongoing-travesty-and-dangers-of-the-prosecution-and-attempted-extradition-of-julian-assange/

3 Hedges explains how Julian Assange also "exposed that Goldman Sachs paid Hillary Clinton $657,000 to give talks, a sum so large it can only be considered a bribe, and that she privately assured corporate leaders she would do their bidding while promising the public financial regulation and reform" (Hedges 2021).

4 Some observers call Obama the "bomber in chief" because he dropped so many bombs on Muslims that the U.S. military almost ran out of bombs. See: https://edition.cnn.com/2015/12/04/politics/air-force-20000-bombs-missiles-isis/index.html

5 See the video: www.mrctv.org/videos/sen-hawley-scary-white-house-working-facebook-remove-problematic-vaccination-posts

6 See: https://twitchy.com/samj-3930/2021/07/18/this-glenn-greenwald-takes-bidens-ministry-of-truth-apart-in-brutal-thread-for-openly-censoring-what-they-deem-covid-misinformation/

7 In case the reader is unfamiliar, 1/6, or January 6, 2021, is the day political protestors stormed the United States Capital building in Washington D.C. after a Donald Trump speech.

8 www.reddit.com/r/TheTwitterFeed/comments/omy9ko/barnes_law_rt_caitoz_they_said_we_need_internet/

9 https://twitter.com/asymmetricinfo/status/1402236124114964481

10 In his debate on *Democracy Now* with University of Chicago Law School Professor Geoffrey Stone, a former informal advisor to President Obama in 2008, Chris Hedges argues "If there are no Snowdens, if there are no Mannings, if there are no Assanges, there will be no free press. … the whole debate—traitor or whistleblower—hearing this on the press is watching the press commit collective suicide … And if we don't wrest back this power for privacy, for the capacity to investigate what our power elite is doing, I think we can essentially say our democracy has been snuffed out." He further argues that those who have the moral courage to expose the human rights abuses of those in power face dire consequences, stating, "anybody who reaches out to the press to expose fraud, crimes, unconstitutional activity, which this clearly appears to be, can be traced and shut down. And that's what's so frightening" (see: https://havanatimes.org/latin-america/is-edward-snowden-a-hero-a-debate-with-journalist-chris-hedges-law-scholar-geoffrey-stone/).

11 See: https://web.stanford.edu/dept/spec_coll/uarch/exhibits/Narration.pdf; https://news.stanford.edu/pr/97/970108prisonexp.html; www.newsweek.com/stanford-prison-experiment-age-justice-reform-359247; www.britannica.com/event/Stanford-Prison-Experiment

12 The actual quote, "Academic politics are so vicious precisely because the stakes are so small" is often attributed to Henry Kissinger. However, Harvard political scientist Richard Neustadt is quoted as saying, "Academic politics is much more vicious than real politics. We think it's because the stakes are so small." Others argue that Wallace Sayre, in "Sayre's law," made a similar statement about academic politics being so bitter. See: R. Keyes 2013. *The Quote Verifier.* New York: St. Martin's Press.

13 See the documentary film *Century of the Self* at www.youtube.com/watch?v=eJ3RzGoQC4s

14 The first author, based on anthropological evidence and studies on non-human animals, would argue that other non-human animals also possess the capacity for agency, at least to the same degree as humans.

15 My colleague David Gladstone is credited with this story on Pretty Boy Floyd, Woody Guthrie, and criminals.

16 www.woodyguthrie.org/Lyrics/Pretty_Boy_Floyd.htm

17 See observations 23 and 24 at https://founders.archives.gov/documents/Franklin/01-04-02-0080

18 www.history.com/news/when-america-despised-the-irish-the-19th-centurys-refugee-cris

19 For example, in the 1970s Americans thought of magic carpet rides when thinking about the Middle East, while today many people think of planes crashing into buildings and wide-eyed terrorists blowing things up. Same goes for the Japanese prior to WWII, Germans in WWI, Africans during slavery, Native Americans during westward expansion, inner-city kids during mass incarceration, Irish and Italians during first waves of immigration, and so on. The key, first dehumanize people, then you can do whatever you want to them. And just as advertisement and public relations (propaganda) convinces us to buy things that won't make us happy and vote for politicians that don't support us, it also convinces us to violate the rights of our brothers and sisters.

References

Becker, Howard S. 2018 (1963). *Outsiders: Studies in Sociology of Deviance*. New York: Free Press, an imprint of Simon & Schuster, Inc., [2018] ©1963.

Butler, Smedley D. 2018. *War is a Racket*: original edition. [Place of publication not identified]: Dauphin Publications.

Cohen, Stanley. 2011. *Folk Devils and Moral Panics: The Creation of the Mods and Rockers*. Abingdon, Oxon: Routledge.

Donnelly, Jack. 2013. *Universal Human Rights in Theory and Practice*. Ithaca: Cornell University Press.

Durkheim, Emile. 1958. *The Rules of Sociological Method*, trans. S. A. SoloVay and J. H. Mueller. Glencoe, IL: Free Press, 68–69.

Eisinger, Jesse, Jeff Ernsthausen, and Paul Kiel. 2021. "The Secret IRS Files: Trove of Never-Before-Seen Records Reveal How the Wealthiest Avoid Income Tax." Propublica. June 8, 2021. www.pro publica.org/article/the-secret-irs-files-trove-of-never-before-seen-records-reveal-how-the-wealthi est-avoid-income-tax

Freud, Sigmund. 1922. *Beyond the Pleasure Principle*, authorized translation from the second German edition. London. Hogarth Press and Institute of Psycho-analysis.

Goode, Erich, and Nachman Ben-Yehuda. 1994. *Moral Panics: The Social Construction of Deviance*. Cambridge, MA: Blackwell.

Greenwald, Glenn. 2020. "The Kafkaesque Imprisonment of Julian Assange Exposes U.S. Myths About Freedom and Tyranny." Greenwald.substack.com. December 30, 2020. See: https://greenwald.subst ack.com/p/the-kafkaesque-imprisonment-of-julian

Hawdon, James, John Ryan, and Laura Agnich. 2010. "Crime as a Source of Solidarity: A Research Note Testing Durkheim's Assertion." *Deviant Behavior* 31 (8): 679–703.

Hedges, Chris. 2021. "Chris Hedges on the Ruling Class' Revenge Against Julian Assange." *Sheerpost*. May 7, 2021. https://scheerpost.com/2021/05/07/chris-hedges-on-the-ruling-class-revenge-agai nst-julian-assange/

Hedges, Chris. 2021. "Sheerpost." June 11, 2021. https://scheerpost.com/2021/06/11/chris-hedges-jul ian-assange-and-the-collapse-of-the-rule-of-law/

Hedges, Chris. 2021. "Bless the Traitors." *Sheerpost*. July 12, 2021. https://scheerpost.com/2021/07/12/ hedges-bless-the-traitors/

Herman, Edward S., and Noam Chomsky. 2010. *Manufacturing Consent the Political Economy of the Mass Media*. Johanneshov: TPB.

Iannone, A. Pablo. 2001. *Dictionary of World Philosophy*. London: Routledge.

Johnson, Jake. 2020. "'Looting of America by Big Corporations': Progressives Appalled as Senate Unanimously Passes Largest Bailout Bill in US History." *Common Dreams*. March 26, 2020. www. commondreams.org/news/2020/03/26/looting-america-big-corporations-progressives-appalled-senate-unanimously-passes

Nelson, Steven. 2021. "White House 'flagging' posts for Facebook to censor over COVID 'misinfor-mation'." *NY Post*. July 15, 2021. https://nypost.com/2021/07/15/white-house-flagging-posts-for-facebook-to-censor-due-to-covid-19-misinformation/

Parsons, T., H. H Gerth, and C. Wright Mills (Eds. and Trans.). 1946. *From Max Weber: Essays in Sociology*. New York: Oxford University Press.

Rappeport, Alan. 2021. "Wealthiest Executives Paid Little to Nothing in Federal Income Taxes, Report Says." *New York Times*. June 8, 2021. www.nytimes.com/2021/06/08/us/politics/income-taxes-bezos-muskbuffett.html?campaign_id=9&emc=edit_nn_20210609&instance_id=32552&nl=the-

Reiman, Jeffrey H., and Paul Leighton. 2020. *The Rich Get Richer and the Poor Get Prison: Thinking Critically About Class and Criminal Justice*. London: Routledge.

Russell, Bertrand. 1945. *A History of Western Philosophy, and Its Connection with Political and Social Circumstances from the Earliest Times to the Present Day*. New York. Simon and Schuster.

Sweney, Mark. 2009. "Barack Obama Campaign Claims Two Top Prizes at Cannes Lion Ad Awards." *The Guardian*. June 29, 2009. www.theguardian.com/media/2009/jun/29/barack-obama-cannes-lions

United Nations General Assembly. 2013. "Report of the Independent Expert on the promotion of a democratic and equitable international order, Alfred-Maurice de Zayas." www.ohchr.org/Docume nts/Issues/IntOrder/A-HRC-24-38_en.pdf

Weber, Max, Hans-Heinrich Gerth, Charles Wright Mills, and Max Weber. 1965. *Politics as a Vocation.* Philadelphia: Fortress Press.

Weber, Max, Guenther Roth, and Claus Wittich. 1978. *Economy and Society: An Outline of Interpretive Sociology.* Berkeley: University of California Press, 53.

Chapter 4

The Sociological Imagination and Human Rights Policing

Introduction

This chapter introduces the sociological imagination as a tool for understanding people and the world they inhabit. We offer a brief discussion on the meaning of the sociological imagination and how to use it when looking at people and their community. Since we, as authors, serve the discipline of criminology, we offer examples from criminology to discuss how to use the sociological imagination to understand the world beyond the subjective experiences of our own lives. The chapter strives to impart the sociological imagination to readers so they can use it to better understand their communities, and further, better protect and serve them while conducting police work. We continue with a discussion on the relationship between storytelling and human rights. People have the right to tell their own stories, but oftentimes, academics, journalists, and various media platforms strip people of their voice and right to self-representation, and this often leads to violations of human rights and dignity. In the end, we ask you to apply the lessons learned in this chapter on the sociological imagination to a member of the community with whom you experienced a negative interaction, or with someone you have arrested, to tell the community member's story and life circumstances.

An Invitation to the Sociological Imagination

Perhaps the term sociological imagination misleads the reader into thinking of some grandiose, highly pretentious academic concept professors use to make themselves sound unique or smart. It's a term that once belonged to the sociologist but now rightfully belongs to more thoughtful people regardless of their formal educational levels and fancy degrees. Many sociologists have never used the sociological imagination, and many, we suspect, still never fully grasp what the concept means. But many sociologists claim to have and use it. Indeed, given the anti-intellectual climate that dominates much of the liberal arts today, perhaps the sociological imagination should be renamed the "thinking imagination" or the "transcendent imagination," or to employ the abused and highly overused term the "critical imagination." The failures of sociology in fulfilling the promises of the sociological imagination breaks the heart of the romantic scholar, as it does the first author, who received his doctoral degree at the New School, and largely agrees with the renowned sociologist Peter Berger who asserts:

> The kind of sociology I learned at the New School ... has very little to do with what goes on with sociology today, except for the background—when people talk about the classics ... (Sociology) suffers from two diseases. One is ... "methodological fetishism." Whatever cannot be put in terms of statistical data is not real. That is crazy ... they do not help

DOI: 10.4324/9781003220282-5

you to understand society as a whole. The other disease is ideological … the sociology of identity … politically left or center and culturally anti-bourgeois … That is unfortunate. Even if my politics were left or center … I would deplore that … most of what people write about is very trivial, such as relationships between X-ray technicians and nurses in a hospital … What these earlier guys tried to understand was: what is our society going through, what is the direction of social change, what is modernity. And about that, you do not get much questioning today.

(Vera 2016, 27)[1]

But we have yet to give new verbiage to the concept so we remain stuck with the "sociological imagination."

To its credit, when sociology mattered, and asked the big questions about the nature of reality, the foundations of knowledge, and the causes of historical change, many sociologists employed that magic of the sociological imagination. Eventually, that imagination spread to the other philosophical disciplines including anthropology, psychology, economics, political science, criminology, and history—at least, to the best scholars within those respective disciplines.

Most importantly, the sociological imagination is a powerful way of thinking about the world, and it's a concept that belongs to the public, not some privileged academics living in the safety of the university. It's a concept that belongs to all people, possesses the ability to empower all people, and provides a powerful way to understand the world beyond our subjective experiences. What's more, we ask you to consider using the sociological imagination in all your police work to advance the goals of human rights policing.

You learned from the previous chapters all about the meaning of human rights, human rights policing social interactions, and the power of human agency as it relates to achieving human rights policing, among other things. Now we invite you to the fruits of thinking in powerful new ways about the world. We invite you to an imagination that will help you better understand the world and the communities you serve. We invite you to a way of thinking that will improve the institution of law enforcement and advance the goals of a human rights policing as we push into the 21st century.

We now invite you to the sociological imagination.

The Sociological Imagination

The sociological imagination allows its possessor to see the world beyond the limited confines of subjective experience. It also allows its possessor to see the world from a perspective other than one's own. In short, it's a perspective for seeing reality beyond your own body and experiences. As Peter Berger stated, "sociology is not so much a field as a perspective and if this perspective fails, nothing is left" (Berger 1992, 18). The intellectual, or thoughtful person does not need a doctoral degree, or any other degree, to employ the perspective of the sociological imagination to think in new and highly creative ways about the world. The sociological imagination belongs to the intellectually curious public, to those who want to better understand the world and their place in it. And if we, as a human species, fail to develop the sociological imagination, then indeed, as Berger says, perhaps nothing is left. We argue that your ability to become even better police officers and law enforcement agents depends on developing the sociological imagination to apply human rights policing to your professional careers.

In 1959, the now infamous sociologist Charles Wright Mills wrote the seminal *The Sociological Imagination* to describe the unique ways sociologists (if they possess the imagination) think to understand the world beyond the private orbit of their lives (Mills 2000). To understand the social world, the individual must look beyond the limited experiences of her life. All of us live within a relatively small part of the world for most of our lives, a cultural milieu (family, friends, work, community) that shapes our beliefs about the world and the values we hold most important. The inevitably limited experiences of an individual make it difficult to fully grasp the world beyond the confines of one's existence.

> Nowadays people often feel that their private lives are a series of traps. They sense that within their everyday worlds, they cannot overcome their troubles, and in this feeling, they are often quite correct. What ordinary people are directly aware of and what they try to do are bounded by the private orbits in which they live; their visions and their powers are limited to the close-up scenes of job, family, neighborhood; in other milieux, they move vicariously and remain spectators. And the more aware they become, however vaguely, of ambitions and of threats which transcend their immediate locales, the more trapped they seem to feel.
>
> (Mills 2000)

As a result, we need a way of thinking to overcome these challenges.

The tools of the sociological imagination help to understand the great structural transformations of our time and the great speed of change occurring in our late-modern world. People who possess the sociological imagination transcend their subjective views of the world based in that cultural milieux to understand both the personal troubles people experience and the structural issues of our era.

The key to the sociological imagination is understanding the relationship between personal troubles and structural issues. The sociological imagination allows us to understand the link between "the personal troubles of milieux and the public issues of social structure."

> *Personal troubles* "occur within the character of the individual and within the range of his or her immediate relations with others; they have to do with one's self and with those limited areas of social life of which one is directly and personally aware."

> *Structural Issues*, on the other hand, "have to do with matters that transcend these local environments of the individual and the range of her inner life. They have to do with the organization of many such milieux into the institutions of an historical society as a whole."

Mills explains that issues are a public matter, a threat to the public order, that often involve a crisis, or contradiction, in the institutional arrangements of society (Ibid).

Understanding the relationship between the individual and her society is essential. Mills says:

> When a society is industrialized, a peasant becomes a worker; a feudal lord is liquidated or becomes a businessman. When classes rise or fall, a person is employed or unemployed; when the rate of investment goes up or down, a person takes new heart or goes broke. When wars happen, an insurance salesperson becomes a rocket launcher; a store clerk, a radar operator; a wife or husband lives alone; a child grows up without a parent. Neither the life of an individual nor the history of a society can be understood without understanding both.
>
> (Ibid)

Or in the case of using the sociological imagination when thinking about crime:

> When a drug market rises, a struggling college student becomes a drug dealer; a tough kid, an enforcer; a poor building superintendent, a lookout; and a dishwasher, a drug kingpin. When a drug market expands, a mother mourns her dead dealer son; a dad laments his drug-using daughter; a child visits a parent imprisoned by the state. When a drug market peaks, an ill-affected sibling becomes a social worker; a storefront preacher, a community organizer; a stay-at-home mom, an after-school volunteer.
>
> (Contreras 2012)

That's the key, understanding, simultaneously, the intimate connection between the individual and society. At any moment, social and historical change can radically alter our biography, and it does all the time. That's the sociological imagination, fully grasping the intimate link between the individual's personal troubles and societal structural issues. It involves constantly looking back and forth between the individual and their structural world. Once we understand the sociological imagination, we need to use it to make sense of both the social world and of those who occupy that world, including the major structural issues that cause the personal troubles people face.

Using the Sociological Imagination

People constantly face problems not of their own making. People also must confront challenging conditions they did not create but must deal with all the same. That is, most of the social problems we experience are beyond our control. Consider some of the major problems we experience like war, unemployment, divorce, crime, and poverty. Let's start with war.

As Mills says, consider war:

> The personal problem of war, when it occurs, may be how to survive it or how to die in it with honor; how to make money out of it; how to climb into the higher safety of the military apparatus; or how to contribute to the war's termination. In short, according to one's values, to find a set of milieu and within it to survive the war or make one's death in it meaningful. But the structural issues of war have to do with its causes; with what types of people it throws up into command; with its effects upon economic and political, family and religious institutions, with the unorganized irresponsibility of a world of nation-states.
>
> (2000)

Structural issues cause our personal troubles. As individuals we must find ways to solve our collectively experienced structural problems. Again, to think with the sociological imagination requires us to understand the intimate link between personal troubles and structural issues.

How about the social problem of divorce? Mills says:

> Inside a marriage a man and a woman may experience personal troubles, but when the divorce rate during the first four years of marriage is 250 out of every 1,000 attempts, this is an indication of a structural issue having to do with the institutions of marriage and the family and other institutions that bear upon them.
>
> (Ibid)

Or look at the problem of unemployment.

> When, in a city of 100,000, only one is unemployed, that is his personal trouble, and for its relief we properly look to the character of the individual, his skills and his immediate opportunities. But when in a nation of 50 million employees, 15 million people are unemployed, that is an issue, and we may not hope to find its solution within the range of opportunities open to any one individual. The very structure of opportunities has collapsed. Both the correct statement of the problem and the range of possible solutions require us to consider the economic and political institutions of the society, and not merely the personal situation and character of a scatter of individuals.
>
> (Ibid)

In other words, looking only at the personal troubles of any one individual will result in the failure to understand, and much less resolve, our social problems such as unemployment, war, and divorce. Rather, these are structural issues that transcend the individual and go beyond the private orbit of any one individual's life.

Similarly, diagnosing a social problem as the result of individual pathologies or structural issues can be readily applied to poverty. In many major American cities, child poverty rates reach absurd levels close to 45 percent. That's nearly half of all children living in poverty in one of the richest countries in the world. When child poverty rises in excess to such levels, it would be a major fundamental error, a complete misdiagnosis, to assign blame strictly at the individual level. While individual counseling and education might help people cope with their troubles, the problem of poverty is the result of structural conditions, that is, something is wrong in the institutional arrangements of society—the problem is largely structural. If we really wanted to solve problems like crime and poverty, we would make changes at an institutional level to ameliorate our social problems.

Perhaps interesting to police officers, using the sociological imagination helps to understand the problem of crime. Looking at relatively high crime rates in many American cities, it becomes apparent that the problem of crime transcends the individual. While "good" and "bad" people sit on both sides of the law, personal troubles inadequately explain the causes of crime. For example, large cities like Chicago, New York, New Orleans, Los Angeles, among many others, have relatively high crime rates. If only a dozen people were committing crimes in each of these cities, we would look at the character of those dozen individuals and examine their personal troubles. We would examine their family upbringing, education, diet, mental health, and perhaps their personalities, among other things. With so few people committing crime in a city, the problem probably relates to personal troubles of the individual that require a solution for that individual. On the other hand, high crime rates indicate that the problem of crime is probably a structural issue, that is, located in the institutional arrangements of society. We need to look at where the contradictions exist within our various institutions that cause crime to emerge in otherwise great American cities. Put differently, crime is a structural problem that requires change at an institutional level.

Taken from a true story, consider the case of Jerome, a young lad in legal trouble over extensive truancy, talking to a sentencing specialist in his office. A sentencing specialist in Michigan named Tim feels it his duty to council the eighth-grade male named Jerome who recently skipped 120 out of 180 days of school. Tim lectures Jerome for almost an hour about the middle-class virtues of attending school, respecting authority, doing homework, getting jobs, and obeying rules and laws. The young Jerome sits patiently slumped in the chair on the other side of the huge desk with eyes glossing over, looking past the sentencing specialist's head. When Tim finishes with the stern "tough love" talk, Jerome leans over, asking, "Are you finished?" to which Tim replies in the affirmative. Jerome then goes on to state, "You must think that I am stupid. Just because I don't go to school does not mean I'm stupid." Jerome continues,

> Listen, I stand on the corner of 68th and Simpson Avenue to blow a whistle every time I see a cop. When I blow the whistle, all the dealers flock to safety. They return once the cop leaves. These dealers pay me $200 a day, tax free. Why would I give this up to go to school so that when I graduate, I'll work 52 weeks a year for poverty wages?

As the surprised sentencing specialist listens, the counselee becomes the councillor as Jerome confidently points out, "I make more money than most college graduates. I'll probably retire before you." Jerome, now looking deep into the eye of the sentencing specialist, asks, "Now who is the fucking stupid one?"

While we, as authors, do not necessarily condone the often self-destructive life of working in the informal drug economy, we argue that a society unable to provide Jerome a proper response is a failed society. That is, if we cannot offer a realistic alternative response to Jerome's reasoning, perhaps we as a society are the ones failing Jerome.

Once I, the first author, interviewed a junior in high school who frequently challenged authority, resisted formal educational settings, refused to work poverty-wage jobs, and preferred to work in the informal drug economy. I told him becoming at least mediocre through "legitimate" avenues was rather easy, almost anyone, barring major physical or mental limitations, can go to college, get a regular job working 40 or so hours a week, buy a house and fill it with stuff, purchase a car, pay bills, and, in short, be mediocre. He replied, "Who the fuck wants to be mediocre?" "Good point," I thought to myself.

Touché

It's obvious most of us want to be something more, to spread our wings and become something important and meaningful, and we can't all do it the same way.

It's interesting that most questions on the problem of juvenile crime start with "Why do kids cause so many problems for adults?" This clearly shows bias in our thinking. If we were objective, we would also consider: "Why do adults cause so many problems for kids?" More importantly, when juvenile crime rates reach high levels, we must use the sociological imagination to figure out the structural issues that are creating the personal troubles for so many people like Jerome. People need money to survive in a capitalist society—and one way or another, they will get it, even if they must find creative ways when the legitimate paths fail them or seem ineffective. Despite all the well-meaning teachers, counselors, social workers, school police officers, D.A.R.E programs, psychologists, and other professionals, there have always been kids like Jerome, and there always will be, despite our best efforts, unless changes are made at the structural level. Further, if we as a society keep putting people like Jerome in jail for decades, we will simply, and cowardly, lock the problem away without dealing with the causes of the problem. What's more, putting kids in cages, as the first author has personally seen while teaching in Brooklyn juvenile jails, often turns peaceful kids into violent adults.

It's important to note, looking at how structural issues cause personal troubles does not absolve Jerome of his actions. Jerome makes the decision to work in the informal economy every day. But closer inspection into the structural conditions Jerome faces shows that he makes a rather rational decision, or at least one that makes sense, given his current situation and available opportunities. After all, looking at it in the context of culture, crime is a creative cultural solution to collectively experienced structural problems (Young 2011). The creation of the underground informal economy is just one type of cultural response. If there were just one or two people like Jerome in our cities, we would need to look closely at Jerome, his school, diet, family, and mental state of being, among other things. But when so many young people turn to the informal economy, we must ask, what kind of society produces such a world where young people turn to the informal market in the dangerous streets of the city? The problem is structural.

In short, the sociological imagination allows us to understand the decisions people make while operating under specific historical circumstances, structural conditions, and cultural milieux. It allows us to better make sense of how and why people make decisions, and never in a vacuum, but as a response to social conditions they did not cause.

When we look at the causes of street crime, it becomes obvious that its causes relate to a problem in the structural arrangements of society, problems impossible for police, teachers, and social workers to solve, despite their best efforts.

Yet, police find themselves constantly blamed for a problem they cannot possibly solve.

In the end, in order to understand structural problems, we need to look at how they impact the personal troubles of the individual. Simultaneously, in order to make sense of personal troubles, we need to look at the structural conditions that gave rise to them.

Once the budding intellectual grasps the link between the individual's personal troubles and societal structural issues, we begin to understand what causes the problems of the world, and how they impact the individual who must deal with a world she did not create. This allows us to develop another essential tool of the sociological imagination, to which we now turn.

Verstehen: The Actor's Point of View

Borrowing from the classical theorist Max Weber, the anthropologist Clifford Geertz once stated:

> Believing, with Max Weber, that man is an animal suspended in webs of significance he himself has spun, I take culture to be those webs, and the analysis of it to be therefore not an experimental science in search of law but an interpretive one in search of meaning.
>
> (Geertz 1973, 5)

Geertz directs us toward the search for meaning: the main pursuit of the anthropologist, the scholar of culture, but, more importantly, perhaps the greatest pursuit for all human beings. While understanding the link between personal troubles and structural issues remains important to *understand* the world, it does not provide *meaning* to the world. To grasp meaning, we need to understand the subjective meanings humans give to their own lives, how they view reality, experience emotion, and make sense of their worlds. Enter the Weberian concept of *verstehen*.

Verstehen involves seeing the relationship between experience and understanding. It involves grasping the subjects' own perspectives, seeing and experiencing the world from another human's point of view. *Verstehen*, as Max Weber put it, involves "empathic or appreciative accuracy (that) is attained when, through sympathetic participation, we can adequately grasp the emotional context in which the action took place" (Weber 1978, 5). Although we can never fully understand each other (Tucker 1965), understanding someone else's point of view requires us to, as close as possible, adopt their perspectives and see the world through their eyes and experiences. Developing empathetic understanding also requires us to understand that social action occurs within very specific historical circumstances and structural conditions. To better understand people, and develop empathy to see the world from their point of view, we must understand that people respond to these circumstances and conditions not of their own choosing.

For example, many criminologists attempt to explain the "criminal" based solely upon socially prescribed categories such as race, class, sex, gender, and ethnicity, among many other possible variables. These criminologists write "theories" explaining the criminal without ever getting to know one, never going to their schools, neighborhoods, boxing gyms, grocery stores, churches, or community events. They learn all about the criminal from the comfy confines of their university or, often times, safe neighborhoods and suburban homes. They do this using elaborate statistical formulas parading as a sad charade of science to explain people they know little about to advance their careers.

Imagine, and this happens frequently, a sociologist or criminologist attempting to explain you, a police officer or law enforcement agent, without talking to you, attending your community events, talking to your friends or family, experiencing your joys and sorrows, experiencing everything you encounter on the job, or knowing your past experiences, including family upbringing, childhood neighborhood, and life challenges. They cut you up into socially prescribed categories, variables, and reduce you to mere numbers, a fractured self, divorced of your humanity.

Insulting?

Can they ever know you?

Even if they spent time getting to know you, will they every really know you?

Can anyone outside of those closest to you?

Yet, many academics claim to know you just as they know the "criminal" using variables punched into their laptops and stories other people tell about you. Should people trust social scientists who make claims to "authoritative knowledge" about police officers without ever taking the time to know them? Should people trust their theories? Similarly, should people trust their claims to knowledge about "crime" and "criminals" they know little about? It's well known that their theories fail, and often fail miserably, including their failure to predict the massive drop in crime in the 1990s (Young 2012).

In short, despite the quantitative world of the sociologist and the positivism of the criminologist, human beings remain an unknown entity.[2] Human beings cannot be known through quantifying them with endless categories and variables in the same way that one can know Newton's three laws of motion or the periodic table (Tucker 1965). Just like categories such as race, class, sex, gender, income level, and other socially prescribed categories do not define us, or allow others to understand our full humanity, people cannot understand another human through quantification, or any other measures known to civilization.

The golden rule, "Do unto others as you would have them do unto you," or simply, treat others as you want to be treated. Don't do to others what some arrogant academics do to you. To find meaning, we need to discover it on our own, through connecting with people, understanding the colors through which they experience the world. In other words, we shouldn't judge others until we have walked in their proverbial shoes and experienced, as closely as possible, their joys and sufferings, hopes and desires, loves and losses, triumphs and failures, struggles and challenges, personal troubles and moral convictions, and their incredible potential for human agency even in the toughest of circumstances.

Weber's concept of *verstehen* helps to understand the world from the actor's point of view. Once we, as closely as possible, feel their feelings, experience their experiences, know their forms of knowing, we will achieve a better, but still incomplete, understanding of their complete humanity.

To understand the individual based on the storytelling of others, or in stereotypes that dominate popular discourse, or in media fabrications that become part of the popular imagination, is to take away the individual's humanity and right to self-representation. The following inter-view between a news reporter and an American of Japanese descent reveals the problem of stereotypes, or the stories others tell about other people, even positive ones:

REPORTER: But I suggested that compared to the black and the Chicano, the Japanese-American has it made. He can get a job, a place to live.

AMERICAN OF JAPANESE DESCENT: It's a situation where I think the question is not material, making it in terms of economics, but a question basically of human dignity. … We've been set in a certain category and many people argue, "Man you got a good stereo-type, you got a stereotype that gets you apartments where you don't have to pay a cleaning deposit because you're so goddamn clean." That's our stereotype. But, it's an infringement, it's a violation of our human dignity because they don't view us as individuals, as human beings. We fit into a certain category, we fit into a certain box. That's how they view us.

In telling such stories about others, human beings lose their humanity, and no longer enjoy the power to tell their own stories that belong to them. Instead, they lose their full humanity when divided into categories, cut into variables, placed into prefabricated typologies, and forced into pre-written narratives.

Verstehen can be understood as a radical form of empathy. It does not necessarily lead to compassion, but rather gives us the ability to understand how other people experience their world. It gives us access to the meanings of human experience from the experiences of beings who exist outside your shell of a human body.

Yet, law enforcement agents and criminal justice professionals serve and police individual community members they know little about, except from, perhaps, media-fabricated moral panics as well as academics writing about people they don't personally know.

Becoming a better police officer and criminal justice professional requires understanding the perspective of others, being able to see and experience the world, as closely as possible, from the other's point of view. We believe that using *verstehen*, or grasping the subjects' own perspectives, will serve the goals of human rights policing.

Stories tell us much about people, but not what we necessarily think. People tell stories in ways that express how they want to view themselves, and further, how they want others to view them. That is, people make up fictions, sometimes unconscious truthful fictions[3] and sometimes purposeful fabrications, that tell us how they view themselves and how they want to be viewed.

Stories about the "self" belong to the storyteller, who attempts to convey their impression of the self, perhaps the best sense of self, to those to which they tell their stories. And every-body has the right to tell their own story.

The Stories We Tell

The conversation below says something about how we construct identities through telling stories:

WOMAN ONE: Well do you know that thing Benedict Anderson says about identity?

WOMAN TWO: No.

WOMAN ONE: Well, he's talking about like, say, a baby picture. So you pick up this picture, this two-dimensional image, and you say, "That's me." Well, to connect this baby in this weird little image with yourself living and breathing in the present, you have to make up a story like, "This was me when I was a year old, and then later I had long hair, and then we moved to Riverdale, and now here I am." So it takes a story that's actually a fiction to make you and the baby in the picture identical to create your identity.

WOMAN TWO: And the funny thing is, our cells are completely regenerating every seven years. We've already become completely different people several times over, and yet we always remain quintessentially ourselves.[4]

This excerpt depicts a scene of two women at a coffee shop speaking about individual identity. The conversation explains how we make up stories, often fictional tales, to connect our past to our present, and in doing so, maintain a sense of identity. People construct stories to connect, for example, a photograph or an image of ourselves from the past with who we are now. Anderson's concept of identity refers to the fictional stories we create in the telling of our own past experiences. It's not as simple as conscious self-deception or attempts to deceive the other, but rather what our memories do to connect our past selves to our current self. In large part, this happens through the telling of our experiences to both ourselves and others. We literally speak our reality, and further, our identity into existence, that is, our identities are socially constructed through the medium of storytelling (Berger and Luckman 1966).

Humans are the makers of stories and the products of them (Smith 2003). The narratives we constantly tell make and direct our life (Ibid). Christian Smith argues that human animals understand who we are and how we ought to live through the narratives we give our stories, and further, locating ourselves within the larger narratives and metanarratives that we hear and tell as well as what is heard and told about us (Ibid). We human animals make stories and are at the same time made by our stories (Ibid). A narrative "is a form of communication that arranges human actions and events into organized wholes in a way that bestows meaning on the actions and events by specifying their interactive or cause-and-effect relations to the whole" (2003, 65). Narratives seek "to convey the significance and meaning of events by situating their interaction with or influence on other events and actions in a single, interrelated account" (2003, 65). Narratives have a point; they explain and provide meaning to "events and actions in human life" (2003, 65). They have characters (both subjects and objects of action), structured plots, and convey significant points that explain or reveal something important, where the storyteller selects specific events from the past that serve as the vehicles of commentary and meaning-making (2003). Only certain "happenings are important to recount, … those that render a particular story by emplotting selected elements in a way that conveys the larger intended moral and meaning" (2003, 66). What matters is not the "facts" but rather "the more significant story running through, over, and under 'the facts', the story that itself constitutes what is a fact, what it is that matters" (2003, 66).

Humans fundamentally believe in these stories. Our stories shape our worldview, and further, our understanding of ourselves and the world beyond the small private orbits of our lives—from our worldly perceptions and political views to our self-understanding and understanding of others (Smith 2003).

Professor of Biology Emeritus at Harvard University and social commentator Richard "Dick" Lewontin discusses the problem of people telling the truth to themselves and, for that matter, to researchers (and their surveys, questionnaires, and interviews) in social science research (Young 2011). He says,

> People do not tell themselves the truth about their own lives. They need to create a satisfying narrative out of an inconsistent and often irrational and disappointing jumble of feelings and events (that) leads each of us to write and rewrite our autobiographies inside our own heads, irrespective of whether anyone else is ever privy to the story.
>
> (Lewontin 1995, 24–29)

In an advanced modern world characterized by ongoing and rapid individual and structural changes, telling the truth may not be as easy as it seems. Peter Berger characterizes the present globalizing world as an age of plurality where the individual constantly confronts new choices in just about every area of social life. Even one's sex is no longer determined, but is rather a choice (Berger 1992). Psychologist Kenneth Gergen explains how this increased exposure to pluralism creates a complex and "fragmented" self where individuals find themselves cast into various roles and identities (1992). It becomes increasingly difficult to take all the fragments of the self and piece them together into a coherent whole—a story tied into a neat bow.

Cultural criminologist Jock Young depicts our current moment of history of late modernity as a situation of extraordinary rapid change, contradiction, blurring of realities, creativity, reflexivity, disruption, instability, spatial mobility, pluralism, boundary testing, social disembeddedness, expressivity, excitement, immediacy, and hybridization (2007 and 2011). This picture of modern times says something about how identities form and change throughout the life-span. Young explains how we live in a world where narratives are constantly broken and re-written, values are contested, and reflexivity defines the times (Young 2004 and 2011). A lifetime of broken narratives, Young explains, creates a world where people constantly reinvent themselves as a central life task. Using both fictional and factional tales, people constantly rewrite and reinvent themselves (Ibid). Human actors, he suggests, have the power to rewrite their narratives especially in late modernity, in which people become increasingly conscious of their roles and scripts in society (Ibid). In a world of plurality and choice, nothing is fixed or solid—including the identities of our past and present that we constantly fashion in new and creative ways for ourselves and give off to others.

Yet, people find themselves robbed of their own ability to tell their story, write their narrative, and represent the self. It happens to both cops and criminals, but mostly impacts the marginalized and dispossessed. Perhaps it's time to reclaim our stories from all the academics, journalists, and media platforms that tell the stories of others, robbing them of their own right to self-representation and empowerment.

The Relationship between Storytelling and Human Rights

Whenever we write about the other, we take away their agency.

When we tell stories on behalf of others and represent them from our own point of view, we take away their right to tell their own narrative, their own sense of being, their own ability to represent themselves and spread their wings. Even in the social sciences, mainly sociology and anthropology, scholars write the stories of other people, often poor and marginalized people, with a colonial gaze that depicts the "other" according to our own ideological outlook and prejudices. The liberal sociologist romanticizes members of the informal economy as rebellious heroes finding, despite their self-destructive lifestyles, creative ways to overcome historical circumstance and structural subordination. The conservative criminologist depicts the "criminal" as some poor, wretched, mindless character completely lacking in agency, a byproduct of biology and culture. Street gangs, the focus of police attention, become characters, along with cops, in the narrative of the streets that represent the "other" as always poor, humiliated, lacking agency, morally bankrupt, and without history. They become fragmented into variables (e.g., race, class, gender, income), stripped of their biography, removed from history, ripped from their cultural milieu of work, church, family, school, community, and leisure. They become one-dimensional beings incapable of resistance or transgression, reduced to subjects to be represented, controlled, dominated, and scapegoated for social problems. The system uses them up and purges them out, discarded to the wretched slums or modern-day penal colonies. The humiliation of poverty gets coupled with the humiliation of representation, one that takes away the last remnants of respect for the poor and policed.

What stories have criminologists used to portray the "criminal" in the popular imagination? The "father of criminology" Cesare Lombroso argues in his classic book *Criminal Man* that, "At the sight of that skull, I seemed to see all of a sudden … the problem of the nature of the criminal—an atavistic being who reproduces in his person the ferocious instincts of primitive humanity and the inferior animals" (Lombroso 1911, xiv–xv). Ultimately, the genetic makeup of an individual, the shape of his skull or the shape of her body, causes, or determines, criminality. The notion of atavism argues that one's outward appearance, or physiology, creates savages predisposed to crime. Similarly, later criminologists would associate crime to ethnicity (Irish, African), race, class, and poverty, among other characteristics. These positivistic views still remain prevalent in much of criminology today, even though the terms have changed.

The criminologist gazes upon the corporal body of the underclass individual as a somatic zone of theory-making, the fat body and large cranium predisposed toward criminality, laziness, addiction, dependency, aggression, pleasure-seeking, and irresponsibility. The wide eyes and tawny, dark skin demonstrate a body deserving of distrust, a body capable of rape and aggression. The body becomes a somatic symbol of representation for criminologists to tell stories of the underclass, of everything the good and decent are not, with their low-riding pants and disrespect for authority. In classic Jungian psychology, "Projections change the world into the replica of one's own unknown face."[5] As Jock Young puts it,

> It cannot be an accident that the stereotype of the underclass: with its idleness, dependency, hedonism and institutionalized irresponsibility, with its drug use, teenage pregnancies and fecklessness, represents all the traits which the respectable citizen has to suppress in order to maintain his or her lifestyle.
>
> (Young 2011)

These bodies find themselves depicted in the boring, dry manuscripts of the "professional experts," like the criminologist, just as the journalists, never knowing the humans and their bodies being depicted, repeat the narrative that becomes part of the popular imagination. The body of the other, the underclass, is now devoid of its human qualities, just as the criminologist cut the corporeal anatomy of the specimen into pieces to predict the criminal, to know its predisposed ways. The dehumanized body, now walking the streets trying to claim respect in a world that denies it, finds itself questioned and pushed against the wall. The police touch these bodies with gloved hands and tasers. As the colonial gaze becomes more physical, more real, the officer fondles and dominates the body, putting chains on it on the way to its cage.

The underclass, poor, marginalized, and dispossessed rarely get to tell their own stories. We silence their voices, control their narratives, control their bodies, control their movements, and often, control their thoughts into the "right" way of thinking. Eventually these bodies and their faces, the making of folk devils, are paraded all over nightly news, further justifying their domination, subordination, and abandonment into the physical and metaphorical periphery of social life.

What's worse, the marginalized underclass often internalizes these stories others tell about them into their own consciousness. Eventually, the marginalized often adopt these stories others give to their lives as part of their narratives in the telling of their own stories. In what some scholars call internalizing the logic of oppression, marginalized groups often believe in the stories others tell about them: poor, minority people are aggressive, wild, uncontrollable, ignorant, violent, lack industry, and hold no value for education, among other things. When we listen to the marginalized tell their own stories, the stories of others dominate their narrative. Put differently, the poor and marginalized adopt the ideology of oppression in the telling of their own stories. This internalized oppression happens when marginalized groups internalize and adopt into their consciousness, they believe the negative views and stereotypes other, usually more powerful, people tell about their lives.

For example, when I, the first author, was conducting research on violence in the inner-city, I interviewed a young lad primed to take over a block in his neighborhood. His brother, recently killed over a few dollars in his pocket, was captain of the block. Before his death, he defended the block and offered protection to members of the community, including getting groceries for the elderly and serving as an informal positive mentor for the younger kids on the block, though activities such as encouraging them to read books and play sports. The kid was devastated that his brother was shot down but promised to take his brother's place taking care of the block. I told the kid that he might meet the same fate, and urged him to reconsider. He stated, "I don't care, I'm going to defend my people. If the cops attack me, fuck them. If these other dudes on the block want to get me, fuck 'em too, I'll defend myself. We wilding out here, and we need some type of protection, I'll defend my people, even if I die, and I know I will." This is a classic case of the marginalized internalizing the stories that other people who are often more powerful tell about them. In this case, it's a young man, at no fault of his own, internalizing the logic of oppression while living in one of the many urban apartheid slums of the inner-city. In other words, he now believes, and further recites, the language of internalized oppression when telling his story.

Meanwhile, in many major cities where the marginalized live in segregated urban colonies, young women and men excluded from access to proper security, healthcare, education, well-paying jobs, and dignity and respect also internalize their rage at each other. The following excerpt reveals how marginalized people in the inner-city often turn rage and violence on each other (e.g., black on black crime).

> The inner-city represents the United States' greatest domestic failing, hanging like a sword over the larger society. The only force sustaining this precarious sword is the fact that drug dealers, addicts, and street criminals internalize their rage and desperation. They direct their brutality against themselves and their community rather than against their structural oppression.
>
> (Bourgois 2002, 30)

Telling the stories of other people, often from the viewpoint of those powerful enough to write about other's stories, such as academics, journalists, media influencers often result in such devastating consequences. In turn, the subject of these stories internalizes them into their consciousness and, further, sometimes manifest these stories into violent, self-destructive actions. Police can't stop the marginalized from internalizing these stories, and they can't prevent other people from telling these stories from the language and ideology of oppression. And they can't stop the violence and crime that results, in part, from these stories. Police officers can, however, give voice to members of the community they police, and they can allow others to give voice to their own narratives. Further, police officers and criminal justice professionals can reject the stories other people tell about the poor, the heavily policed, and other marginalized groups. If we don't reject such stories told about others, these stories become part of a shared narrative. Resisting these shared narratives of oppression serves as one way of exercising our agency. Police can be better than those storytelling academics, journalists, and media pundits.

Storytelling and the Double Consciousness

People tell stories about police officers without knowing them. The stories often depict police as rabid racists, "wannabe" fascists, little Nazis, control freaks, petty bullies, self-righteous ego-tistical maniacs, and white supremacists that hurt, kill, and murder with impunity.[6] These stories, especially when people with large audiences tell them, become part of the dominant discourse.

Some academics serve as armchair theorists who often attempt to dominate the narrative and tell the story of police officers just as conservative criminologists do to the underclass. A scholar at a university in the West Coast once told me that he believes all police are bound to a system of violence and oppression, all white people are bound to white supremacy, and all men are bound to toxic patriarchy. This ideological authoritative assertion, he claimed, is backed by research.

The scholar's claim that all cops are bound to violence and oppression, all people with a certain absence of melanin in their skin are bound to white supremacy, and that all men are bound to toxic patriarchy (apparently including Malcom X, Fred Hampton, Gandhi, the Dali Lama, and Martin Luther King) not only denies people of their story, but engages in the most irresponsible and misleading representations of millions of people. The meaning of terms become lost. White supremacy becomes reduced to anything that disagrees with orthodox thought, or the socially correct way of thinking. The strange American concept of "white" becomes synonymous with oppression. The concept of a white person remains unclear. Who exactly is white: Cubans? Jews? Hungarians? Indians? Spaniards?[7] When do they, or did they, become white, if ever? And to whom did they become white, or not? What about mixed-race people? Or what about creoles? Who gets to define a person's race? The fact that race has no biological meaning is completely ignored.[8]

Did this academic study every man, white person, and police officer all over the world—billions of people? Did he interview what every woman and non-white person believe to be true about all men and white people? Did he interview what all people think about police officers in their community?

The various cultures of the world, many of which exist in the United States, are completely ignored. The various ways different cultures interpret the concept of men, white people, and even police officers, also remain entirely ignored. Does this scholar speak for all women in every culture about men? Do all Buddhist women view their husbands as being bound to toxic patriarchy? Does he speak for the Pakistani woman who fell in love with an Indian sol-dier who saved her life and gives his full devotion to her every day? Does he speak for the Kenyan mother who left a powerful impression on her white son to always respect and honor women? Does he speak for the Indonesian wife who absolutely feels all the love and ador-ation of her Australian husband? Does he speak for the black Nigerian man who sees all the beauty in the world in his hero and best friend, a white woman from rural Wisconsin, who also happens to be his wedded partner? Does he speak for the Cuban kid thankful to police who saved his life after experiencing anaphylactic shock from a red ant attack?[9] The arrogance of speaking on behalf of billions of people from so many different countries, cultures, histories, languages, religions, and ethnicities is entirely absurd.

In this claim, men and white people, a rather ill-defined concept with no global consensus, from ethnicities and cultures all around the world lose their culture, history, and right to give voice to their own experiences. What's more, the claim demonstrates a peculiar, strange hubris of a scholar writing about billions of people he knows nothing about. It offers no room for debate, no discussion, no self-doubt, no other voices, only pure moral righteous certainty—social reality is rarely filled with such certainty and lack of nuance.

While such things as patriarchy and privilege exist, denouncing an entire group of people without knowing them seems reductionistic, deterministic, anti-intellectual, and since based on ideology, not scientifically credible.[10] What's more, the fact that most people—regardless of their race, class, gender, sex, ethnicity, and so on—use the same institutional hierarchical structures of power and patriarchy to dominate and exert power over others is entirely ignored.

This type of storytelling serves as an anti-intellectual response to the more hateful character depictions of the "other," the underclass, the labeled, the represented, the controlled. Some people, including professors, are doing to cops what orthodox academics, journalists, and politicians have done to the underclass for centuries. It's the flip side of the proverbial coin.

Many police officers probably find such views, the stories told about the police officer, unfair and perhaps unjust. It takes away the ability for police officers to give voice to their own narrative.

Academics and journalists take away the voice of both police officers and criminals when they tell their stories in the narratives of the streets. They take away the ability of people on both sides of the law (and there are good and bad people on both sides of the law) to give voice to their own human experiences and identity. Such stories strip people of their ability to write their own story, shape their own narrative, and represent themselves.

The great sociologist Du Bois wrote how black people experienced a sense of otherness and exclusion in the United States (Du Bois 1903). It's a problem that perhaps all people experience in a highly divided, hierarchal society.[11] Du Bois said:

> It is a peculiar sensation, this double consciousness, this sense of always looking at oneself through the eyes of the other, of measuring one's soul by the tape of a world that looks in amused contempt and pity. One ever feels his two-ness, an American, a Negro; two souls, two thoughts, two unreconciled strivings; two warring ideals in one dark body, whose dogged strength alone keeps it from being torn asunder. The history of the American Negro is the history of this strife—this longing to attain self-conscious manhood, to merge his double self into a better and truer self. In this merging he wishes neither of the older selves to be lost. He does not wish to Africanize America, for America has too much to teach the world and Africa. He wouldn't bleach his Negro blood in a flood of white Americanism, for he knows that Negro blood has a message for the world. He simply wishes to make it possible for a man to be both a Negro and an American without being cursed and spit upon by his fellows, without having the doors of opportunity closed roughly in his face.

(1903, 2–3)

While Du Bois was describing the feelings of being both an American and a black person, other people experience this feeling of two-ness. For example, many immigrants experience this sense of two-ness today with feelings of being both a member of their original culture and a Britain or American.[12] It's a sense of becoming "othered" with two conflicting identities that others impose upon you. This experience largely happens when others deprive you of your own story. It happens when people silence your voice and tell your story for you.

To what extent do you experience the feeling of two-ness?

Sociologist Danny Kessler explains how this feeling happens when others tell stories that make you feel like an outsider, inferior, and the "other," because of your social class, immigration status, sexual orientation, or racial and ethnic identity.[13] In today's political climate, perhaps police officers also sense this feeling of two-ness. But the questions must be asked:

How often do you tell stories that turn others into your inferior?
How often do you make people feel like outsiders?
How often do you "other" other people based on some category?

If police officers want to tell their own stories, and shed the stories others have written about them, then police officers and law enforcement agents need to simultaneously reject the stories others tell about the poor, the underclass, the marginalized, the dispossessed, the folk devil, and those deemed criminal. If we want to tell our story, let others tell theirs, regardless of their media and academia-tarnished representations.

Human rights policing largely depends on police officers taking the first steps to question the stories others tell about the people they serve. Human rights policing requires law enforcement agents to take the time to listen to others tell their story and allow community members to control their own narrative about their stories. It requires allowing people the ability to write their own scripts and give meaning to their own concerns, emotions, and experiences.

The ability to tell one's own story, we believe, is a human right. Taking away the right of the "other" to tell their story violates the human rights of the other.

Human rights policing involves law enforcement agents talking to the people they serve, hearing their stories, understanding their experiences, and taking seriously their focal concerns.

If, as Mark Twain said, "Travel is fatal to prejudice, bigotry, and narrow-mindedness," then hearing the stories others tell about themselves is fatal to the same limitations of mind.

Knowing people's stories provides insight into their humanity bursting with colors and imagination, hopes and dreams, fears and desires, love and jealousy, agency and struggle, beauty and ugliness, and contradictions and struggles for redemption. We all exist in that same world where we grasp for ontological meaning and existential purpose as we reach high to realize the essence of our being. They, like us, are full, complete beings with their own stories. This realization makes *verstehen*, radical empathy, possible. It's an important process leading to the understanding, and application, of human rights policing.

Thirty Years of Policing a Foreign Community

The sociological imagination, what a unique perspective to see the world and grasp reality. It allows us to look at problems around us and make sense of them. It requires us to distinguish between personal problems and structural issues and to ask if people are the sole makers of all their personal problems. Or have people been thrown into a situation through no fault of their own?

To those of us in law enforcement with no extensive training in the social sciences, the problem of crime, our daily concern, can seem challenging to understand. I came to that conclusion after many years of wearing the badge. No matter how many people we put in jail, crime remains. That became very apparent to me after continually arresting drug traffickers. There was always someone to take his place in the business. That was true of ring leaders as well as low-level dealers slinging dope on a corner. That was even true of homicides. You could put a cop on every corner, homicides were still not going down. So, we knew that as police officers we could not solve the problem of crime.

But we still had a job to do.

And we do the job every day.

We must now ask, how can we, as police officers, understand the causes of crime? I am not going to offer you that explanation just yet, as the first author provided some sociological insights already. But I will tell you a little bit about my story just to give you a perspective on the sociological imagination.

At least for me, trying to understand crime as a police officer was like a Martian coming to earth (not influenced or filtered by our culture), seeing crime, and the society in which it takes place, and trying to figure out the factors accounting for crime.

The story starts when my parents decided to seek political asylum, or refuge, in the United States from the political and economic situation in Cuba. I was only 14 years old when we arrived, set up a household, and enrolled in school. I graduated high school and attended Louisiana State University (LSU) and, after one semester, decided to enroll in the demanding University of New Orleans (UNO), eventually receiving a bachelor degree in sociology. I went on to graduate school in the same discipline. Like most students, I was undecided on a major when starting my studies at the university. But as I looked around American society, I realized that I knew little about it. In those early years, my world consisted of associating with other Cubans and remaining immersed in Cuban culture. So, I wanted to know about my new country. What better discipline than sociology to learn its institutions and its people!

After leaving the sanctuary of the university, I met a New Orleans Police Sergeant on a recruiting drive who asked me the big question, "Son, do you want an adventure or a job?"

Of course, you know the answer.

I took the adventure.

I soon found myself sworn in and assigned to what was called at the time The Vice Crimes Section before attending the police academy. It was a total shock; I had never before seen what the men in the squad called "ladies of the night." I found myself going undercover, approached by those ladies in the New Orleans French Quarter, arranging sex for money. As I went through other legal steps to follow official protocol, the rest of the squad would come in and arrest the women in question. It was then that I thought I was beginning to understand my new country. There were many times after the arrests that I asked these women about their families and their lives. What they told me was as much about their lives as it was about American society. Those stories often highlighted the structural problems these women faced. There was one in particular that stood out in my mind. I will call her Amanda to protect her privacy.

Amanda got busted for prostitution in one of my undercover assignments in the Quarter. Her problem was that she had several prior arrests not just for prostitution but also theft, shoplifting, and possession of cocaine. She was actually facing the three strikes and you are out law in Louisiana. So, she called a short time after her arrest wanting to know if she could cooperate and reduce her legal problems. I accepted and met her in our office in police headquarters. Her cooperation eventually led to the arrest of several sex and narcotics traffickers. She ended up pleading guilty and receiving a suspended sentence and time on probation. Amanda's story was moving. She grew up in northern Louisiana in a troubled family. Her mother was an alcoholic while her father constantly abused her sexually and physically. She never completed high school as she was always running away. She had been addicted to heroin, cocaine, and other synthetic drugs. There were times that she could function and get a job, only to fall off after being pressured by the many sex traffickers she knew. When asked why she fell for those sex traffickers, she responded that they were the only ones who would bail her out of jail every time she got arrested. Amanda was certainly traumatized as she broke down in tears several times during her interviews. Amanda faced many structural problems that were beyond her control.

After the academy I was assigned to a police district for about three years and eventually made my way to a specialized unit called "Special Operations" Tactical Unit. Our mission was to work in plain clothes to "jump crimes in progress." Although the unit worked citywide, we concentrated in the high crime area. I now had over three years on the job working in uniform and answering calls for service, but still did not get to know the so-called criminals.

Working in Special Operations changed everything.

I soon realized that the easiest crime in progress to "jump" was narcotics transactions in the many street corners of our city. After working the unit for a while, and making numerous arrests, I quickly learned that much more success could be achieved by "cultivating informants" from those very people I was arresting. Of course, the best informants were often the most successful criminals. The best informants brought me much closer to knowing the culture found in those areas of the city with the highest concentration of poverty. Although I eventually transferred to The New Orleans Police Departments Narcotics Unit working the big kilo cases, the tactical unit concentrated on street-level dealers.

As I cultivated informants, from street dealers to wholesale dope users, I learned all about their lives. Having my cell phone number, they constantly called me with information about what was going on in those street corners. Of course, these informants were no saints, as they would often call to knock out their competition for customers in the corner.

The pace of the Tactical Unit was fast and furious. Eventually I came to have a very strange feeling when I began to analyze my role from the perspective of that little Cuban boy with a very curious mind who at the age of 14 entered a new, and strange, world.

That boy grew up in a very different culture. And in his new culture he had only known mainly white middle-class folks. That world consisted of his dominantly white neighborhood, his high school years in a segregated school, and his college years with mostly white students. Outside of Cubans and white Americans, I only personally knew two other black people well. One was a black kid who became my best friend in Havana. But in my formative years, I did not notice that Jorge was considered black. Only later, after reminiscing about my friend, did I realize that Jorge was black. Outside of Cuba, the only other black people I knew was the black family in my neighborhood. Other than those two relationships, I had little knowledge of the black culture in New Orleans, especially those with a high concentration of poverty. What's more, I had never seen poverty prior to my arrival in the United States.

Having that sense of "two-ness" discussed in this chapter, I began to look at my role as a police officer from the perspective of a Cuban immigrant. Although I was American (I was a citizen), I was also Cuban.

I felt this sense of being out of place; I felt like I did not belong policing these black communities; I realized I policed a community almost completely foreign to me; I began to experience myself as a mercenary.

After all, these people were completely alien to me. I came to their neighborhoods, picked someone to inform me about what was going on in their lives, and who was slinging dope (something very normal for many), for me to lock them away.

It felt peculiar; it was strange.

There were two informants who stood out from the many others I came to cultivate over my many years in the Narcotics Unit. These were two brothers whose specialty was not only dealing cocaine but also "ripping off" other dealers when there was an opportunity. I came across them on a lucky day during a surveillance. I purchased cocaine from them, resulting in their arrest for possession with the intent to distribute cocaine. The brothers posted bail shortly after their arrest and called me to meet them. I was not surprised by the call; I had now come to know the narcotics business in the city of New Orleans.

I knew the informant game.

My partner and I met the two brothers in a secluded part of the city and learned that they were well entrenched in the city's cocaine infrastructure. They were willing to cooperate for help with their charges as they were multiple offenders.

Then our relationship began.

The day after the meeting, they called telling me that they were at a corner of the city and were watching a street dealer dealing crack cocaine to costumers. They provided every detail a narcotics officer needed to set up a surveillance and make an easy arrest.

Over the next two or three years the two brothers continued their roles as informants long after their case was settled. There were times I was riding around and spotted the two brothers driving. When I stopped them to talk, sometimes I would find that they had thousands of dollars in their possession and at other times they had nothing and would ask me for money and offer information on an easy-to-catch street dealer. But, over time, they contributed to many cases in which they introduced me, in an undercover capacity, to cocaine dealers, resulting in multiple arrests and the seizure of large amounts of cocaine.

So, I got to know those two brothers well.

I met one of their cousins (also involved in cocaine trafficking) and their mother. Their mother was a sweet older woman, a school teacher, who had no idea of what their two sons were doing and my relationship to them. I met her several times when I picked up her two sons at their house. I am not even sure that she realized that I was a police officer. I got to know the family and the hurdles the mother faced raising two kids alone (there was no father present) in a segregated part of the city where narcotics trafficking was common and very visible. I got to see them as human beings living very difficult lives and adapting for survival. And for that little Cuban boy who became a police officer, this unique look and insight into the world of narcotics traffickers and the people in it gave me access and a perspective that any sociologist would envy. It was this experience of seeing the humanity of the people I was policing that I took with me when I finally left the Narcotics Unit. I realized that if I treated those people with genuine respect, if I listened to their stories with compassion and empathy, I could deal with them much easier. I kept that perspective even as I retired after 30 years.

But I must say, in the context of the real world, I was there doing the job the society had asked me to do—combat narcotics traffickers.

Now to the subject of the sociological imagination.

Having unprecedented access to those engaged in crime gave me a unique perspective often not accessible to researchers and sociologists. That perspective is even more unique from the 14-year-old boy from Cuba who grew up to become a police officer in an American city.

You might say that I was the guy from Mars looking at crime.

What does use of the sociological imagination require?

The sociological imagination asks us to consider the personal troubles people face under the structural conditions that they did not cause.

The sociological imagination requires us, as police officers, to ask if all the personal troubles people face result strictly from the personal shortcomings of the people we meet (as a law enforcement officer). Or perhaps we can better understand their personal troubles from within the context of the structural impediments they face. After all, people find unique, sometimes creative, and other times self-destructive ways to solve their structural problems.

One factor here to consider is the concept addressed earlier in the chapter: agency versus determinism. How many of those people I encountered on the job used their agency to rise above those structural impediments?

While some people cope with their structural conditions, others use their creative agency to find solutions to their collectively experienced structural problems, and sometimes these solutions require transgression and law violation.

How might people find solutions to their structural problems entrapped in a world of poverty, geographical isolation and segregation, poor failing schools, poor physical infrastructure, high unemployment, substance abuse and addiction, high incarceration rates tearing through family ties and role models, poor access to health care, as well as constant police presence in stop and frisk mode? The proverbial "pull yourself up by your bootstraps," hard-work-and-go-to-school cliché simply doesn't apply to many people facing extreme structural conditions of exclusion.

All the problems of the world can't be fixed by telling people to go to school and work hard. It works for some, but clearly not for many who face overwhelmingly challenging conditions.

Those children growing up under those circumstances face such powerful structural impediments that the hard-work-and-go to school motto does not apply.

But they must find a solution anyway.

It is mostly the structural impediments those people face, not personal issues, that create the conditions for crime. In fact, many of them use agency to rise above their personal shortcomings and thrive in the world of narcotics trafficking and other behaviors we label criminal to achieve some economic success and high status.

My sociological imagination allowed me to analyze my observations and determine that the issues I saw relating to crime stem from the structural impediments those people faced rather than their personal shortcomings.

We can't understand the decisions people make unless we see the world from their point of view, taking into consideration the structural issues they face all happening within specific historical circumstances. That sociological imagination helped me use my human agency, and human agency allowed me to understand, and practice, human rights in all my relationships with people, including in the policing profession.

Suggested Activities

Activity One: The Double Consciousness, Two-ness, and Human Rights Policing

Recall W. E. B. Du Bois' concept of the double consciousness, otherness, and feelings of two-ness in the statement below.

> It is a peculiar sensation, this double consciousness, this sense of always looking at oneself through the eyes of the other, of measuring one's soul by the tape of a world that looks in amused contempt and pity. One ever feels his two-ness, an American, a Negro; two souls, two thoughts, two unreconciled strivings; two warring ideals in one dark body, whose dogged strength alone keeps it from being torn asunder. The history of the American Negro is the history of this strife—this longing to attain self-conscious manhood, to merge his double self into a better and truer self. In this merging he wishes neither of the older selves to be lost. He does not wish to Africanize America, for America has too much to teach the world and Africa. He wouldn't bleach his Negro blood in a flood of white Americanism, for he knows that Negro blood has a message for the world. He simply wishes to make it possible for a man to be both a Negro and an American without being cursed and spit upon by his fellows, without having the doors of opportunity closed roughly in his face.

As discussed in Chapter 4, while Du Bois was describing the feelings of being both an American and a black person, other people experience this feeling of two-ness when they are "othered" with two conflicting identities imposed upon them. These feelings of two-ness happen when others make you feel like an outsider, inferior, and the "other," because of your social class, immigration status, sexual orientation, and/or racial and ethnic identity, or some other imposed category. Now we ask you the following questions.

- How often do you tell stories that turn others into your inferior?
- How often do you make people feel like outsiders?
- How often do you "other" other people based on some category?

Please discuss your response to the above questions and its implications for advancing human rights policing.

Activity Two: Interviewing a Community Member

We discussed humans as storytelling animals and are now equipped with a budding sociological imagination that helps to understand the intimate link between personal troubles and structural issues. Now it's time to hear the stories of a member of the community you police. We want police officers and law enforcement professionals to see the world from the perspective of the people they serve. This assignment asks you to talk with a member of the community, preferably someone with whom you experienced a negative interaction, or arrested. Find out their story, ask them about some of their life experiences, the events and decisions that shaped their life as well as the circumstances around them. Let them tell their own story, frame their own narrative, and represent their own experiences. We also recommend opening up to the community member, tell them your own story as well, to find some commonality that unites the human experience.

In this activity, discuss your findings with your fellow colleagues and friends. Explain what you learned and experienced about the community member from their—the "others"— point of view. Be sure to use your sociological imagination throughout your discussions. Finally, please discuss how building rapport with members of the community, and seeing the world from their point of view, might help achieve the goals for human rights policing.

Notes

1 For the full interview, see: Vera, Hector. 2016. "An Interview with Peter L. Berger: Chamber Music at a Rock Concert." *Cultural Sociology* 10 (1): 21–29.
2 Positivists in the social sciences generally believe that human animals can be understood through the same scientific methods as other non-human animals and plants. If the scientists collect enough data and use rigorous research methods, they can predict and fully explain human behavior.
3 It's not a lie if you believe it to be true.
4 This excerpt is a script from the philosophical movie *Waking Life*. Retrieved from www.script-o-rama.com/movie_scripts/w/waking-life-script-transcript-linklater.html
5 This line refers to Carl Jung's concept of the shadow.
6 It's important to note that police officers in the United States, in general, possess far more social status than many other countries around the world that have less respect for police officers. Based on my travels around the world, police officers outside the Western world, especially outside the United States and United Kingdom, lack social status and respect. In some places, police are seen of the lowest members of society.
7 If one goes to Cuba, Israel, Hungary, India, and Spain and asks, respectively, a Cuban, Jew, Hungarian, Indian, and Spaniard if they are "white," one might be surprised with the responses.
8 While race is a social fact, it's biologically meaningless.
9 In case the reader is wondering, all of these scenarios are true.

10 As Peter Berger stated, "A science that becomes an ideology is no longer a science." Although I would argue that it's absurd to claim that sociology or criminology (along with any academic discipline in the liberal arts) are classed as a "science." All of the social sciences are ideological.

11 Danny Kessler, Adjunct Professor at John Jay College of Criminal Justice (CUNY), reminded me of the importance of Du Bois's concept of the double consciousness. His discussion of the double consciousness in his forward to my manual *Social in the Age of Discontent: A Manual for Sociological Thinking* (Kendall Hunt Publishing, 2021) inspired this section relating the concept to the stories people tell about both police and policed.

12 Our Cuban family experiences this sense of two-ness, or feelings of being both Cuban and American, with two different and sometimes conflicting identities, especially in such a highly divided world in the United States.

13 See Danny Kessler's forward to Peter Marina's *Social Problems in the Age of Discontent: A Manual for Sociological Thinking* (Kendall Hunt Publishing, 2021).

References

Berger, Peter L. 1992. "Sociology: A Disinvitation?" *Society* 30 (1): 12–18.

Berger, Peter L., and Thomas Luckmann. 1966. *The Social Construction of Reality: A Treatise in the Sociology of Knowledge*. Garden City, NY: Doubleday.

Bourgois, Philippe. 2002. "Understanding Inner-city Poverty: Resistance and Self-destruction Under U.S. Apartheid." In *Exotic No More: Anthropology on the Front Lines*, edited by Jeremy MacClancy. Chicago: University of Chicago Press, 30.

Contreras, Randol. 2012. *The Stickup Kids Race, Drugs, Violence, and the American Dream*. Berkeley: University of California Press.

Du Bois, W. E. B. 1903. *The Souls of Black Folk*. New York: Dover Publication.

Geertz, Clifford. 1973. *The Interpretation of Cultures*. New York: Basic Books.

Gergen, Kenneth. 1992. *The Saturated Self: Dilemmas of Identity in Contemporary Life*. New York: Basic Books.

Lewontin, Richard. 1995. "Sex in America." *The New York Review of Books* 42 (7): 24–29.

Lombroso, Gina, and Cesare Lombroso. 1911. *Criminal Man, According to the Classification of Cesare Lombroso*. New York: G. P. Putnam's sons.

Mills, C. Wright. 2000. *The Sociological Imagination*. Oxford, UK: Oxford University Press.

Smith, Christian. 2003. *Moral, Believing Animals: Human Personhood and Culture*. New York: Oxford University Press.

Tucker, William T. 1965. "Max Weber's Verstehen." *The Sociological Quarterly* 6 (2): 157–165.

Weber, Max. 1978. *Economy and Society: An Outline of Interpretive Sociology*. Berkley: University of California Press.

Young, Jock. 2004. "Voodoo Criminology and the Numbers Game." In *Cultural Criminology Unleashed*, edited by Jeff Ferrell, Keith Hayward, Wayne Morrison, and Mike Presdee. London: Glass House Press, 13–29.

Young, Jock. 2007. *The Vertigo of Late Modernity*. Thousand Oaks: Sage.

Young, Jock. 2011. *The Criminological Imagination*. Cambridge: Polity.

Chapter 5

Engaging with the Community on Human Rights

Introduction: Soulful Policing

The jazzman riffs "EE-yah!" and "EE-de-lee-yah!" to a transcending Kerouac in constant search of this abstract but certain thing called *it*.[1] Before him it was Dickenson[2] reaching that inevitable moment of *it* until the fly buzzes and Emerson's[3] search for *it* in the nature and soul of the universe. Sometimes *it* finds symbolic expression in places like Melville's whale,[4] Gilman's yellow wallpaper,[5] or Faith in Hawthorne's Young Goodman Brown.[6] Sometimes *it* is in the production of the thing itself like "Jack the Dripper's" abstract expressionism where Pollock must be "*in* my painting, ... to let it come through."[7] But *it* is never the thing itself; it's not the finger but where the finger is pointing, not the symbol but the soulful meaning given to that symbol. Sometimes *it* is forced upon the tortured innocent soul like Sugar in Bambara's "The Lesson"[8] or Huck Finn's confrontation with hypocrisy in his adventures with Tom Sawyer where "a sound heart and a deformed conscience come into collision and conscience suffers defeat."[9] At other times *it* is a desperate search that must continue, no matter what the end might bring like at the end of Hemingway's double-barreled shotgun.[10] Sometimes people never see *it* while at other times *it* slaps them in the face and they still can't recognize *it*. *It* remains an underlying theme that the great novelists, essayists, poets, beatniks, creatives, mads, artists, intellectuals, and those who push to move beyond and search for something more attempt to achieve.

And that is the challenge of becoming aware—the search for *it*—our soulful call to arms, and our renewed promise to police with the sociological imagination. We need a "sociological police imagination" that allows us to become aware of the people we protect and serve. It's the quest for something more that moves beyond the tenets of science. Soulful policing is the search for *it*—the ability to become aware and find out more—about the communities we police. What is their *it* and how can we become aware of their awareness? What does community policing look like from their perspective? We must replace our tired traditional police lenses of an old world long gone with a renewed police imagination that allows us to better understand the constantly changing communities we serve to advance human rights policing.

How do the people in communities that law enforcement agents serve understand human rights as it applies to policing? How might they perceive the best practices for police to ensure all community members enjoy the human rights that naturally belong to them? If police officers want to understand their communities from beyond a traditional police lens, they must put on their sociological caps and go into the community—Chicago School Sociology style.

The 1920s Chicago School Sociology: Getting Dirty

Sociology is the systemic study of human social life (Mooney 2020). The philosophical discipline concerns itself with order and disorder, functionality and dysfunctionality, organization

DOI: 10.4324/9781003220282-6

and disorganization, social integration and disintegration, rule-making and rule-breaking, crime and obedience, transgression and conformity, and societal stability and transformation. It's a field of inquiry that loves the enchantment and chaos of the city, and the inner-workings of social life in both the public and private sphere as well as in all the hidden cracks and crevasses of urban jungles where human life finds its most creative realizations. Chicago in the 1920s became the harbinger of American sociology. It was the place where sociologists began to investigate social problems and crime from first-hand observations inside the city. Chicago served as the greatest natural social laboratory of the world to study human social life and its problems. The Chicago School scholars focused on exploring social life first-hand, venturing into the city to investigate social problems such as worker exploitation, inequality, crime, homelessness, prostitution, drugs, addiction, cults, and industrial slave labor, among other things.

Although dominant historical memory ascribes men as the leading Chicago School theorists, it was the women of Jane Addams and Ellen Gates Starr's Hull House in Chicago that created some of the best ethnographic scholarship in Chicago (Mooney 2020). The "mother of ethnography," Annie Marion MacLean's impressive work focused on women's working lives where she authored two brilliant articles—"Two Weeks in Department Stores" (1899) and "The Sweat-Shop in Summer" (1903)—in the *American Journal of Sociology*. Maclean used her body as a research instrument to collect first-hand data about social life working in a department store, and, later, a women's summer sweat-shop in the city (Ibid). Maclean argues that "only by 'participating' in the world of the 'toiler' that 'meaning' can be given to their experiences" (Mooney 2020, 138). In other words, to understand the world of others, one must become, to the extent possible, fully immersed into that world. One must participate in the world of others, and live under their conditions, to understand how people make sense of their own experiences and give meaning to their lives.

Other female Chicago theorists such as Frances Kellor and Katharine Bement Davis delved deep into the city to investigate crime and criminal justice policies in Chicago, challenging some of the dominant theories in a largely male-centered discipline (Mooney 2020). The Chicago School theorists of the Hull House produced some of the greatest work in feminist criminology as well as radical criminology, challenging structures of power and inequality. Their work on wage slavery, gendered exploitation, the miserable conditions of the working class, women and immigrant experiences in the industrial factories, women in prisons, and housing conditions of the city's Bohemian immigrants, among many other topics, produced some of the most impressive scholarship rivaling the great works of Frederick Engels' *The Condition of the Working Class in England in 1844*, among others (Ibid). At the time sociology mattered, and these early Chicago School women advocated for social reform that pushed for new social policies to ameliorate the social problems of their time. This could not be done through abstract theory and grand theorizing from the armchair of the office. Rather, they could only accomplish this impressive insight into social life by going out into the community to not only observe, but participate in the social worlds of the communities they wanted to understand. The social policies they advocated for were based on the real experiences people faced in the communities they wanted to understand. Their courage, and moxie, to go out into the city, proved to be some of the best work in sociology even to this day.

Unsurprisingly, the men of the Chicago School received the most credit for the pioneering work of American sociology. Chicago of the 1920s was the heyday of sociology, when sociology mattered and advocated for real material change. The idea was to first acquire knowledge from the real world, and then use that knowledge to change the world. As Marx pointed out, the goal is not to simply interpret the world, but change it.

The Chicago theorist Robert Park glanced at his students famously stating:

> Go and sit in the lounges of the luxury hotels and on the doorsteps of the flophouses; sit on the Gold Coast settees and on the slum shakedowns; sit in the Orchestra Hall and in the Star and Garter Burlesque. In short, gentlemen, go get the seat of your pants dirty in real research.[11]

Chicago served as the laboratory to investigate social life, and for these Chicago School theorists, the world was their oyster. They went into the community to study gangs, dance halls, ghetto life, brothels, hobohemia, delinquent youths, dilapidated neighborhoods, slums, and immigrant neighborhoods, among other people and places.

In short, if you want to know about the social world, what are you doing in a classroom? Get out and get the seat of your pants dirty. Go to the corner bars, brothels, jazz clubs, boxing rings, juke joints, churches, underground nightclubs, street corners, factories, retail stores, neighborhood bodegas, schools, and the very places where people live out their lives. If you want to know the world, you're not going to get it in books, news, media, or anywhere else. In other words, you need to go out and experience it yourself. Talk with members of the community and experience their world from their perspective. Participate in community life and talk with its people to learn how others give meaning to their experiences.

Learning about the community from their perspective, and further, learning how community members make sense of their own life and give it meaning, serves as a crucial step to advance the goals of human rights policing.

What you find might surprise you.

My experiences in a tongue-speaking Afro-Caribbean church in Brooklyn and sleeping in homeless shelters in New Orleans serve as two examples of learning about communities from first-hand experiences.

Tongue Speakers and Religious Fanatics in Brownsville, Brooklyn

One day, my history student from John F. Kennedy High School in New Orleans invited me to attend a Sunday church service at Beacon Light Temple located in a neighborhood called Gentilly fairly close to the school.

I was intrigued.

Not because I was interested in attending church or participating in any formal religion; I've always been religiously unmusical. I was surprised because he was a tough kid in the school, and neighborhood, who seemed to have no fear of danger, including confrontations with police or other dangerous characters of the proverbial street. He feared, however, God.

At the time, I was writing my Master's Thesis on youth resistant subcultures of New Orleans focusing specifically on how young urban black women and men find creative, and sometimes self-destructive, ways to overcome their collectively experienced problems of social and economic exclusion. Much of my writing consisted of discussing new modalities of transgression within postmodern subcultures, including how fashion, style, and other cultural symbols serve as creative vehicles for resistance and transgression. But in the background, always in the background, stood the pillar of the black church. I decided that perhaps one day it would serve as an excellent topic worthy of exploration.

Meanwhile, I was intrigued with the idea of tough inner-city kids fearing God but not men with guns, on either side of the law. I also wanted to always support my students, something in short supply for many of these inner-city lads living in what many scholars refer to as American Apartheid.

One Sunday early afternoon, I walked into that church composed mainly of working- and middle-class New Orleans black residents engaged in a particular type of religious fervor.

It was an unfamiliar sight, almost shocking.

People were outside the pews spread all over the church engaged in what seemed to me rather bizarre behavior. Some people were speaking in a strange, rhythmic but incoherent language while others jumped up and down in a sort of religious ecstasy. Some people were passed out on the floor while others bent backwards and forwards with tears flowing from their eyes.

A church usher spotted me awkwardly staring at the crowd near the entrance and kindly directed me toward one of the church pews. The crowd seemed to no longer form a congregation; it unraveled, blew up, and reformed too many times to call it any congregation. It was an intense moment of collective solidarity mixed with deeply lonely, highly individualized personal moments. The woman next to me bellowed in some sort of despair that cracked through the barriers of pain beyond pain, which allowed her to rejoice. She found her moment and collapsed in delight with not a movement more. A jumping man fell from his feet and desperately clamored, crawling on his hands and knees to some seemingly invisible object. Everyone clamored, striving to reach beyond the body and beyond the performance of rituals and gestures, with all the prostrating and collapsing, and the shouts of strange nonsensical words. The individuals consumed in this collective nomic isolation engaged in the wildest of acts, gyrating their bodies, rolling their eyes behind their sockets, jumping up and down with fists clenched in the air, while the preacher man up front did not lead but rather orchestrated the melodic yet thumping conduit into a passageway that is easy to suspect leads to some sort of meaning.

I remembered that moment.

Fast forward a couple of years later when I moved from the Big Easy to the Big Apple. While teaching at a school in Brownsville, Brooklyn, I recalled the memorable story of my experiences attending the black church in New Orleans to a colleague. Turns out, this colleague attended a similar church in the notorious Brownsville neighborhood where the famous boxer Mike Tyson learned how to fight.

I must admit my preconceived notions. I grew up in an immigrant Catholic family and was reared in the more progressive Catholic schools of New Orleans where religion remained strictly a private affair. I didn't know how to make sense of the black church or what role it played in the community. As a beginning doctorate student in sociology, I thought, from studying Marx, that religion served as the sigh of the oppressed creature and the opiate of the masses.[12] After all, I thought at the time, poor people from the inner-city need religion to cope with the problems of their lives.

I was wrong.

I was wrong from the beginning of my research.

I was wrong from the very first question I asked a congregation member.

The first question I posed to a congregation member showcased my ignorance. I asked how she first became attracted to this tongue-speaking religion. She looked at me with a wide grin, but a sense of disapproval, stating: "I am not involved in any religion. Religion is for hypocrites. I'm involved in a personal relationship with God, not religion."

I spent months conducting ethnographic research in the Brownsville Church learning everything I could about this previously unfamiliar world. I knew the importance of full immersion into their life, and the necessity to build rapport with church and community members in order to engage in open, genuine, and honest dialogue.

I also knew that if I wanted them to expose their vulnerabilities to me, I needed to expose my vulnerabilities as well.

In talking with the community and church members, I learned all about the history of Afro-Caribbean immigration set in the cultural context of resistance in Brownsville and the promise of the American Dream while living in a rough, excluded, and segregated neighborhood that some church members called a "ghetto" (Marina 2013). The main characters struggled with living in poverty during uncertain times of instability while finding empowerment in religious belief. The actors struggled at the fringes of society, and denied political, social, and cultural capital, they found alternative forms of social and cultural capital as well as personal empowerment. They created a subcultural world that both empowers them and traps them within conservative political and cultural views that serve as further obstacles to liberation. The characters cried on my shoulder as they struggled with spousal abuse. They were tormented when they fell in love with "unequally yoked" partners and held on to progressive feminist thought while negotiating a religion that marginalizes women in patriarchy and domination. They believed in the world of the supernatural to cure spiritual diseases while also believing in science and modern medicine to cure physical ailments.

The characters reflected on me as I reflected on them. They wondered why a secular academic wanted to study them, and they took pity on me for refusing salvation while I frowned at their uncritical religious views, staunch conservatism, and highly judgmental attitudes. I found a sense of disquiet at their views of women's subordination to men as well as their negative views on homosexuality and gay marriage. They found similar feelings of such disquiet at my refusal to believe in the reality of their God and that God's love serves as the only path of redemption. I challenged my own stubborn secular views and my euro-centric system of knowledge that dominates the world of social science and academia to try to understand their world of miracles, tongue-speaking, and spiritual warfare. I marveled at how they maintained charisma and enchantment in a world that increasingly denies it while they wondered why I couldn't see the world through their eyes.

These congregation members were not simply poor people finding ways to cope in a perverse world of structural inequality and exclusion. They did not view themselves poor or vulnerable, no matter how tough their conditions. They also did not view themselves victims or people needing help. They were empowered. They were alive. They were creating something.

They were doing something more.

Through a Pentecostal tongue-speaking community, they developed a creative cultural solution to their collectively experienced structural problems of poverty and marginalization. They found ways to empower themselves in a world that excluded them from institutions that give access to power. They made their own institutions that granted access to power and dignity.

The church members acquired what I call "Holy Ghost Capital," a subcultural "spiritual" capital accumulated in a successful Pentecostal career where members experienced personal strength from speaking in tongues (Marina 2013). In the church, internal status hierarchies emerged where members demonstrated various levels and intensities of commitment to the Pentecostal career. "Holy Ghost Capital" distinguishes members on an internally devised scale of authenticity and social status demonstrating commitment that demarcates core and elite members from the marginal. The unique dialects tongue speakers developed and changed in their Pentecostal career, which they associate with developing "a closer relationship to God," also demonstrated personal status in the community and personal empowerment outside the group. Church members used Holy Ghost Capital offered in the church community to craft and express a unique form of power and identity. Excluded from the dominant institutions, they made their own institutions to acquire status, power, respect, and dignity. This personal sense of empowerment transferred to their life experiences beyond their church and community.

Engaging with members of the community taught me that Pentecostalism is a cocktail of old-world miracles, modern rational thought, and postmodern religiosity having implications for personal and social change. I linked Pentecostalism to culture and the social problems posed in late modernity. To Pentecostals, religion is not merely a private affair, kept in secret of solemn worship behind closed doors. It's a whole lifestyle and a community that has evolved in urban peripheries, urban centers, ghettos and slums, and rural poor geographic spaces around the notion of a personal relationship with a god, and this is of great possible political and social influence. Pentecostals constantly and consciously transform their identity—through this relationship narrative, defying, even if symbolically, their structural locations in history where, under conditions of late modernity, community, family, and work become increasingly destabilized. They refuse marginalization, accepting in its stead empowerment. Many hold stubbornly to conservative social and cultural ideas that contribute to their own marginalization while also refusing labels of being poor and marginalized and embrace Holy Ghost Capital. They contest definitions imposed on them from the dominant culture—including belonging to a religion—and redefine themselves. As Pentecostalism has made its impact in the public sphere, it expands, gets redefined and re-contextualized. Pentecostalism must be understood not just in the realm of religion, but in the sphere of culture. Pentecostalism is a meaningful and creative response—an elaborated solution—to collectively experienced problems. They are grounded in the challenge of making a life in marginal urban spaces—and denied economic, political, and social capital—make meaning and grasp for some clarity while resisting power by creating a unique form of capital—Holy Ghost Capital. In the end, in many marginalized spaces of the city, including in urban churches, people like Pentecostals develop creative cultural solutions to problems that fit well within the universal and historical context of human resistance and struggle (Marina 2013).

The only way to learn this is to talk with the people in the community. It requires becoming aware of your preconceived notions and making yourself vulnerable to previously unfamiliar people to learn about their lives and community.

All of my preconceived notions about the black church melted away as I talked to people and immersed myself in their lives. While I may not ever become part of their community, I admire and respect them, despite our different views of the world. They found a way to survive and prosper under the most challenging of conditions.

Human rights policing requires getting to know the community you serve in a similar way. It requires putting on a different hat, beyond the police cap, to venture into the community you serve to learn what makes the people tick.

Now go out into the community. Get the seat of your pants dirty—Chicago School style. Talk with members of your community, take interest in their personal stories and lives. Use your power as a police officer to advance human rights policing and make the world a better place.

Down and Out in New Orleans: Homeless Shelters of the City

When doing ethnographic research for my book, *Down and Out in New Orleans: Transgressive Living in the Informal Economy* (Marina 2017), I spent the night at homeless shelters. One specific shelter sat near the corners of Clio Street and Oretha Castle Haley Boulevard with a sign that points to the check-in building for the New Orleans Mission. At around 4:30 p.m., people began showing up in relatively large numbers, perhaps 40 to 50 people. Only about two blocks away, beneath the elevated Pontchartrain Expressway near Calliope Street, dozens of people prepared for another homeless evening with scores of their fellow homeless compatriots. I often wondered why people would sleep in these tent camps underneath the interstate ramp rather than stay at the shelter just two blocks away.

Some down-and-out folks arrived at the shelter for an evening meal and returned to the nearby underpass, while others arrived for a night's rest away from the outside elements. A line of men queued for admittance to the shelter. A guy with missing teeth pats down the bedraggled men like a cop does during an arrest.

The entire process of gaining entry was humiliating and degrading. After getting patted down and getting your body fondled, they ask for name, ID, birthdate, medical records, criminal background, drug use, and other highly personal questions.

They finally get to the religious part. Do you believe in God? Do you want salvation? Do you want to turn your life around? Can't you see the error of your ways? And on and on and on.

After the questioning, I was told to sit at a table while my inquisitor enters the data into a computer. After waiting about five minutes, they call me back into the office. Another man tells me to sit at his desk and begins to ask more questions about my faith in Jesus. He drills me about God, why I don't believe (he assumed), the importance of eternity and so on. It was all work to get me into a 21-day program.

It was as if Orwell spoke to me right then and there: "It is curious how people take it for granted that they have a right to preach at you and pray over you as soon as your income falls below a certain level."

Ain't that the truth, I thought.

After about 15 or 20 minutes of questions and a lecture on the importance of faith, he tells me to sit next to another man who asks even more of the same questions before taking my picture. He tells me that everyone must take a shower before going to bed and asks if I need clothes.

In order to sleep at the shelter, one must present a bed ticket to a nighttime bed monitor with the word "approved" highlighted in yellow on the back of the ticket next to the day's date. It is only possible to get this word "approved" highlighted (aside from smuggling in your own highlighter) from a shower monitor who admits the men into the showers and provides them a towel. The shower monitor handed me a towel and watches me enter the shower and bathroom area.

I would prefer not to discuss the shower facilities in polite company.

That evening, at about 7:45, I walked around to the outside of the facility near the weight area. One of the workers scolded me, saying overnight guests are not allowed to walk around the facilities. He ordered me to sit in the chapel area with the rest of the men.

Showers shut down at about 8:30 p.m., bedtime starts at 9 p.m., and lights out at 10 p.m. There are about 75 single-sized bunk beds on the second floor of the warehouse. When you get to your bunk (mine was the top bunk of number E23) one must put on the mattress cover and pillowcase. Some men sit up, many coughing, while others toss and turn. I remember one man told me he did 22 years in the Louisiana State Penitentiary at Angola, saying homeless shelters offer about the same experience. The lights shut off promptly at 10 p.m., leaving the room nearly completely dark. We are only left with our private thoughts while lying awake and listening to the sounds that dozens of men make throughout the night.

I found that sleeping at homeless shelters is regulated and highly structured. Once a person enters the shelter—which must be done by 6 p.m.—the workers completely regulate the lives of the homeless men. They preach to the homeless, tell them all about Jesus and God and salvation, and what would happen if God questions you about where you belong in the afterlife. There was a moment where some well-meaning students from Tulane University handed the men Coke cans with a look of pity in their eyes. It was condescending, even if well-intentioned.

One feels worthless in a homeless shelter, and worse, needy to others who can "save" you. There is nothing more revolting than getting help from people who fancy themselves as your saviors. In many ways, we are fortunate that shelters such as these provide homeless men and women a place to eat and sleep. God bless them, many people would say, perhaps rightly so.

But I'd prefer a night beneath the overpass or in a squat any day, which I did many times.

Once we know more about people, like the homeless, and spend time living like they do, experiencing what they experience, confronting their challenges and humiliations, we begin to see them differently. We begin to realize that, perhaps, giving them tickets might be the legal thing to do, but not the human rights thing to do.

And besides, homeless people do less harm in society than most people in the world, and they are far better for the environment than most of us.

I'm also reminded of the quote, paraphrased here, that the law, in all its majestic objectivity, makes it illegal for both the rich and poor to sleep under the Brooklyn Bridge.

Human rights policing advances the idea to allow all people to enjoy the human rights that belong to them to the fullest extent possible. Human rights policing is also sensitive to institutionally vulnerable people, like the homeless person sleeping on the streets or man selling lose cigarettes in front of a convenient store, and asks us to put down guns and tasers as well as citations and tickets. Once we learn more about their world, like I did, you see the world differently, and you realize how essential human rights is for preserving any form of a decent, civilized society. We believe police can lead the way.

Can you?

Sex Workers, Policing, and City Life: Getting to Know Community Members

(In the two sections that follow, the second author provides two memorable stories discussing his experiences of getting to know the community from his time as a law enforcement agent in the New Orleans Police Department.)

In this chapter we have been talking about how, in order to know a community, one must have first-hand knowledge of the people in that community. This is especially important for police officers who police a community and want to portray themselves as the enforcers of human rights, not just the ones who respect human rights. Getting to know the personal stories of the people in the community, from their perspective, helps achieve that goal.

However, accomplishing this goal was far from a reality when I first arrived on the job. My first assignment, even before attending the police academy for basic training, was called at the time the "Vice Squad." I was sworn in on a Monday morning at police headquarters and told to report to an office in the same building.

So, I did.

I found the office and knocked on the door. A man who appeared to be expecting me opened the door and, after a brief greeting, told me to come back that same night wearing a coat and tie.

Well, I went home and returned that night as told.

I knocked on that same door and was allowed in. There were about eight officers in jeans and T-shirts and another who was a sergeant in charge of the group. The sergeant gave everybody, including me, $300. I took the money not knowing what we were about to do. Then one said, "Ok, Pedro, let's go get some whores." I had never seen what they called "whore" in my life. I supposed they had and would just arrest them. That night, when we arrived on Bourbon Street, the heart of the French Quarter, we parked the unmarked police cars and walked to a bar they suspected of harboring prostitutes. The sergeant came to me and said, "Alright son, sit by the bar and wait for a 'whore' to approach you and offer you sex for money." He directed me to take her to a fancy and expensive hotel on Royal Street and handed me the keys to the room. He further instructed me to have her take the money, disrobe, and open the door so we can come in and arrest her. I said to myself, "Oh my God, this is not going to be easy."

Well, I sat at the bar and observed all the men from the squad sit at different tables and order drinks. Eventually the bartender asked what I wanted. Not sure about drinking on the job, I ordered a hurricane. I started to sip it slowly when a conventionally attractive woman sat near me asking, "Are you looking for a good time?" I said yes and heard all the kinky things she was going to do to me for $100. I looked at the men behind me and they kept motioning me to get on with it.

I was nervous and did not want to do this, so we talked.

She told me that she arrived from out of town, traveled to New Orleans, fell on bad times and resorted to doing sex work. She said I was different from all the men she "dated" and felt good talking about her life with me. She explained how she ran away from home very early in life because of an abusive father who raped her numerous times. As she kept talking, I could see the sergeant motioning me to take her to the hotel. So, finally I told her that I had a room and we walked hand-in-hand like two lovers down Bourbon Street to Royal Street, up the elevator and into the room. Once at the room, she said that I was too nervous, and to take my clothes off and meet her in the bathtub.

I knew I was not about to take my clothes off so I gave her a few minutes in the bathroom and opened the outside door. The men of the Vice Squad came in screaming, "Where is that whore?" I pointed to the bathroom, they opened the door and dragged her fully naked into the room. Then they said, "New Orleans Police, you are under arrest for prostitution, get you clothes on and let's go." The girl looked at me and said, "I trusted you."

Well, I felt two feet tall.

To the Vice Squad officers she was just a "whore."

To me, she was a young woman who fell on hard times, was abused as a child, and needed help to survive in this cold, hard French Quarter where everything and anything has a price, including an intimate bond between two people.

In my conversation with her at the bar, she mentioned that when she came to New Orleans, she wanted to be a waitress. But then she met this man who offered her a way to make plenty of money working the trade.

She fell into it and could not get out.

However, none of that mattered, she went to jail. Later, I found myself in criminal court relating only the story about sex for money.

This story illustrates how a woman's personal story, and the social setting in which she found herself, explains her difficult path toward sex work. Perhaps a society that allows this to happen should be put on trial, not this institutionally vulnerable, but individually strong, woman.

In an economic system based solely on profit, where everything is for sale, including the body parts of human beings, it is not surprising that the most vulnerable find themselves victims to the games of more powerful people in pursuit of profit and gain.

This structural system exists not only in our French Quarter, but in most American cities in which many troubled young women find themselves vulnerable to ruthless men who prey on these women to make plenty of money.

In the six months I spent doing this every night, I always thought there had to be a better way to deal with prostitution than putting the victims in jail.

I've been reflecting on this for years, and thinking about its implications for us as a society and, specifically, for police officers given the duty to arrest such people.

However, there is another story.

The Gay Business Community of the New Orleans French Quarter

After having worked the New Orleans Police Department for over 20 years, I took the Civil Service exam for promotion to lieutenant. Several weeks passed and the results were announced: I was in the first batch of sergeants to be promoted to lieutenant.

The promotion was bittersweet.

I was happy as a group supervisor assigned to the Narcotics Unit, especially since the lieutenant in charge of the unit was promoted to captain a few weeks earlier and sent to the Eighth District—out of my life.

I did not get along with him. He put the lives of police officers in the unit at risk seeking publicity and fame in front of the news cameras every time we made a big bust.

That Friday the official list of promotions to lieutenant arrived with my name on it. I was quite happy until, to my surprise, the list indicated that I was assigned to the Eighth District— exactly where the man I despised was the commander.

I knew a transfer was inevitable, as per department policy, but to the Eighth, why? Certainly, my investigative skills could serve another district better.

But, no, I was going to the Eighth located in the heart of the New Orleans French Quarter.

On Monday morning I showed up to the commander's office asking, "Why did you ask for me? You certainly don't like me and I am not very fond of you either." He looked at me while stating, "Pedro, I looked at the promotion list and decided that you were the best in that list. I need someone like you in this challenging district. Bygones are bygones." Well, I was not so sure about his sincerity. Maybe he enjoyed making my life miserable. So, I started my work as a platoon commander knowing full well a mistake, no matter how minor, would probably cost me dearly.

Everything was going well since I did not see him very often, until one day, when he sent an email directing me to see him. Right then and there I knew he had something on me, even if I could not figure out what it was.

Ready to fight, I showed up to his office.

He greeted me with enthusiasm while asking me to sit down. He said, "Lieutenant, I have a very important assignment for you. I want you to represent the Eighth District in connection with the Gay and Lesbian Business Association here in the Quarter. I have already given them your name so that you can expect an email from them regarding the date, time, and location of their next meeting. You have my and the Superintendent's blessing to initiate any policy change that you recommend."

Well, I left the meeting wondering why he gave me this assignment, and what's more, wondering how I would successfully perform it. Growing up in Latin America as a little boy, I was sheltered from any behaviors that challenged heterosexual normativity. In fact, I knew nothing about LGBTQ+ people or their cultures. Further, I did not personally know any members of the gay and lesbian community, in New Orleans or anywhere else.

Still, like a good soldier, I agreed the assignment and waited for the email.

A few days passed when the email arrived welcoming me to the organization and announcing the date, time, and location of the meeting.

It's important to note that there is a large, and relatively prosperous gay community in New Orleans. In fact, members of the gay community were one of the first people to gentrify the neighborhoods surrounding the French Quarter, especially Faubourg Marigny.

Not only did they have a huge, and wealthy, presence in population, especially in the back of the Quarter, but they also owned many of the businesses along Toulouse and Bourbon Streets.

They also had an annual celebration called The Southern Decadence Festival that attracted national and international tourists. I have worked as platoon commander during the festival.

A bit of context is needed here. Tourists from all over the world travel to New Orleans for its relaxed rules on drinking, partying, sex, and nudity. It's a highly unique city that celebrates debauchery of almost every kind. During events like the world-famous Mardi Gras, people openly drink on the streets, engage in sexual behaviors, flaunt nudity (during Mardi Gras we have a police sign that says, "No nudity below the waist"), use drugs, and pursue almost every kind of deviant behavior. In short, New Orleans, and in particular the French Quarter, is a place where people engage in almost every sexual proclivity and get drunk and high as kites. The Southern Decadence Festival is no exception.

As a New Orleans police officer, I have seen people totally naked having sex on Bourbon Street. However, I had never taken the time to get to know the revelers or the business owners who host them. What's more, all I heard about the gay community in New Orleans consisted of negative stereotypes that did not place the community in a positive light. As a result, I was quite skeptical of the assignment.

The day finally arrived for me to attend the first meeting.

I headed to the location at a bar right on the intersection of Bourbon and St. Peter Street, a corner quite popular in the gay community known as the heart of the "gay" French Quarter. I knocked on the bar door which appeared to be closed for the occasion. A man attired in a suit opened the door and said, "Lieutenant Marina, welcome."

Well, I entered into a crowd of about 30 people, mostly men, applauding me. I said thank you after the man who opened the door introduced me.

I sat down and the meeting started.

For about an hour they talked business about revenues, supplies, employment, and other business-related matters. Then, they opened the meeting for questioning.

And lucky me, the first question was directed at me.

They asked about New Orleans Police Department policies on loud music coming from a bar. I answered that we enforced the ordinance whenever there is a complaint and that we have the equipment to measure the sound. They asked me many other questions, everything from serving "drunks" to patrons not paying their bill. I had been working in the Quarter long enough to have learned all of that. The meeting came to an end and just about the entire membership came to shake my hand and thank me for attending the meeting and answering all their questions.

I returned to the station and considered writing a memo to the captain, but I decided to wait. The next day I was in my office when the captain came in saying, "You have done good. I just received an email from the association telling me how well you performed. They asked me to keep you in that position."

These men immediately left an impression on me. I was particularly impressed with their business savvy and professionalism. My father managed a hotel in the central district of Havana quite popular with international visitors, including Americans. I had not seen such well-mannered, highly cultured, and well-educated people since my days hanging out with my father and his friends at the hotel.

Over the next few months, I attended meetings and developed friendships with some of the bar owners. They often called me to have lunch in the Quarter. We talked about family, politics, and life. We shared personal stories and formed lasting bonds. One of my new friends, another French Quarter business owner, graduated from the University of New Orleans. He, like me, traveled to many cities and towns of northern Spain, places I visited several times to see the land of my ancestors before they migrated to the new world. We shared stories about our lives and loved ones, including our spouses and how we met. He told me about his husband, helping normalize a relationship that I was never exposed to in my past life experiences. We shared our life aspirations, feelings and love for family and friends.

When some of the association members had a police problem, I found ways to help them. I had officers check on them during the night so that patrons and business owners would feel safe seeing a friendly police presence in the bar.

I developed a profound respect for the gay community of New Orleans and was proud to serve them. Any stereotypes that I may have harbored from my socialization into American life vanished, replaced with a love and bond for my new brothers and sisters trying to make a living and survive this, at times, tough life.

Turns out, the captain did me a favor.

But it was this story that paved the way for that next one to happen: a story about a man named Phil. Phil taught me human rights, not in an academic way, but in a highly personal way of the heart. It made me a better police officer. It made it possible for me to help write a book on human rights policing.

Phil the Maître D'

The New Orleans Police Department requires police officers to live in the city, a policy that's existed ever since I can remember. The policy and its enforcement have changed with the political winds of city politics. It never really affected me. I always lived in the city during my 30 years of service. Therefore, I was never held back from preferential assignments, promotions, or a take-home police vehicle. Just the perk of the take-home police car was enough incentive for me.

I always supported that policy. Living in the city made me part of the city. In fact, when assigned to a patrol district, my neighbors appreciated the marked police car parked on the block. They attributed the lack of crime in our neighborhood, called Gentilly, to the presence of that marked unit. Being part of the Gentilly neighborhood, I was always concerned with the city issues such as drainage, garbage collection, and code enforcement. Needless to say, I was also concerned about crime in my neighborhood, even when I was assigned to another district on the other side of town.

I also noticed that my coworkers who lived outside of the city in the suburbs were not as concerned for the welfare of the city, including its citizens. They were alienated from the people and communities they policed. I often heard some officers put the city in a bad light when they compared it to their lily-white suburbs. They did not vote for mayor, city council, or district attorney. They were not involved with the important issues facing the city.

This is all important in light of what we have been talking about in this section. If police officers are to be the enforcers of human rights, they must know, and build rapport with, the people they serve.

I can offer another example of how getting to know people in the community can influence one's perception of marginalized people.

The story begins when I was working as a patrol officer in the Second Police District located in the uptown section of the city. A highly unique food, drink, and music venue opened within the boundaries of the district. They wanted to hire off-duty police officers for what was called "paid details." One of the scions of a very wealthy family with long roots in the city opened the venue, which was a bar and restaurant with a small and intimate stage. An old building was renovated with a courtyard with exotic trees, flowing fountains, and beautiful brick walls. In time, the place came to host very popular entertainers, eventually becoming the place to see and be seen among the city's wealthy patrons. They hired a well-known professional staff, from a world-renowned chef to the city's most revered maître d, a gay man that I eventually came to know well.

After clearing all the paperwork and getting department approval, I arrived at my detail looking for the manager. I was brought to a man with a British accent who presented himself as the manager. He welcomed me and brought me to the offices upstairs to meet the young lady who owned the establishment. I knew of her family and wealth. She lived in a house, more like mansion, in uptown St. Charles Avenue, one of the city's most prestigious addresses. From her office we went to the kitchen where I met the chef who, to my delight, said he would prepare me a dinner. Then we went to the restaurant where I met Phil, the maître d. Phil was a small man with blonde hair, probably close to 70 years old. Phil welcomed me and said that if I needed anything from the bar or restaurant to see him.

I worked the detail twice a week for the next few months. I befriended all the waiters and other staff members over time.

But Phil was a special man.

He was gentle and polite, and the management and patrons alike respected him. It seemed that many of the wealthy patrons dining at the restaurant not only knew him, they actually frequented the establishment because of him. I got the impression that Phil could always find a table for those patrons who knew him well, even when the place was fully booked, which was almost every night. I had the feeling that those wealthy people took good care of their maître d.

Phil also took care of the police officer working every night. He would often look for me outside on a cold night with a cup of coffee. Many times, when I sat down to eat, he would sit with me, wanting to know about my career and family. In turn, he told me that he lived in a fancy hotel on St. Charles Avenue and had no family here in New Orleans. I knew that Phil was gay, but he never mentioned it until several months passed. In talking to Phil, I got the impression that he was a very lonely man. He knew many people, especially very wealthy people, but not closely. He was lonely. When he let me know that he was gay, he did not actually say so. He just mentioned that he had been in love with a man once, but that the relationship did not last and his heart was broken.

One night I arrived at the venue to find out that Phil was sick and had not come to work for several days. I was concerned.

The next day I tracked him down to the Pontchartrain Hotel on St. Charles Avenue. During my shift that day, I went to his apartment at the hotel. After I rang the bell, Phil opened the door surprised but glad to see me.

Phil did not look well.

He lost weight and appeared pale. I entered, sat down, and asked him what was wrong. With tears in his eyes, he said that there was nothing wrong.

I didn't buy it.

I asked him if he was going back to work the next day. When he said no, I said "I am not leaving until you tell me what is wrong." He broke down again while stating, "If you want to know so bad, I'll tell you, I am HIV positive, I have AIDS, and I don't think I have much more to live."

I was shocked. I knew he was gay, lonely, and heard media reports that members of the gay community were a risky population. I left the apartment devastated, not sure what I could do for a friend who was very special to me.

I visited him over the next few days. One day he told me that he wanted to see some friends in Miami and asked me to take him to the airport the next day. I showed up at his apartment, picked him up, and took him to the airport where he boarded a flight to Miami.

A few days passed when he called me on the phone to ask me to pick him at the airport to drive him home. So I did. I picked him up at the airport and drove him to his apartment. Phil did not complain of any pain, but he looked worn out and weak.

Then, the end came.

The next afternoon, right at the beginning of my shift, I went to see him at his apartment only to find no answer. I went downstairs to the lobby and asked the desk clerk about Phil. The desk clerk said, "You don't know? He was taken to the hospital during the night, and I am told he passed away at the hospital."

Unable to hide my sadness, I returned to the station and took the rest of the day off. A man whose friendship I had come to value died.

As time passed, I reflected on my experience with Phil.

First, returning to the idea of getting to know the community and its people, the residence requirement makes sense as officers live in the community and experience the same issues affecting all the neighbors. Seeing the world that community members experience allows officers to see their struggles and triumphs. Officers can serve a community better when they can not only see, but feel and experience, the humanity of its people. They can even better relate to their experiences.

So is my story about Phil.

I got to know Phil as a human being. My closeness to Phil connected me to the community, which helped me build a stronger connection to the gay business community I represented in the French Quarter.

Phil was a charming, caring, interesting, and elegant man. He personified sophistication, and he always wore a smart coat with a loose collar. He was respectful and considerate. Those are the character traits that I now attribute to all people in the community, regardless of race, gender, class, or sexual orientation. This perspective was essential for me as a police officer in making decisions about freedom, life, and death. It became all about human rights, and that process of becoming a human rights-minded police officer started with my relationships with people like Phil. He made me a better police officer, and a better man.

I never thought of police work as a calling. I graduated from college looking for a job when this opportunity came along. I hear many police officers say that they took the job to help people.

Well, perhaps.

As for me, I was just looking for a job. However, helping others was always important to me. Helping others, combined with my sociological background, allowed me to understand the highly complex and nuanced world using the sociological imagination.

Sociology offers many tools to learn human behavior. But, in order to know human behavior, one must know the wide variety of human beings that make up this world. For me, it was Phil who exposed me to the inner beauty of the human soul, and that all members of the community are capable of showing some of the same wonderful characteristics as Phil.

Thank you, Phil. I hope you are looking at me from somewhere and that you are satisfied with what you have done for this police officer who was just looking for a job.

A Police Chief's Perspective on Getting to Know the Community and Human Rights

Chief Benjamin Bliven of the Wausau Police Department offers the following comments on how human rights policing begins with taking initial steps on getting to know the community and, further, building positive relationships with people throughout the community.

In getting to know members of the LGBTQ+ community, I learned more about their opinions and concerns about the law enforcement profession. One concern relates to their perception that young people receive more negative attention from police officers and, therefore, experience more negative contact with police officers. This information coincides with the survey results from our policing task force community survey. People under the age of 30 were much more likely to have negative perceptions of law enforcement. In addition, people who identify as non-heterosexual also had negative perceptions of law enforcement.

Members of the LGBTQ+ community also expressed concerns about how they are treated, especially on the policies and procedures regarding a search of someone who identifies as a member of the LGBTQ+ community.

I have two primary takeaways from these conversations.

First, everyone pays close attention to how law enforcement treats them. Most people share their experiences with police officers with many other people in the community. How we go about our work impacts many people. Further, subsequent conversations within the community after law enforcement contact shapes the opinions and feelings of many community members.

Secondarily, if we do our work correctly, as in uphold and protect human rights, the word will spread rapidly within the community. I believe this is especially true within communities that distrust law enforcement.

On human rights and law enforcement, it is more important today than ever to build positive relationships throughout and across the community. Some of those relationships are easy to build while others may take time. From a human rights perspective, it is incumbent upon police officers to know, understand, and seek relationships with as many people as possible. These relationships break down barriers (both perceived and actual) and help us achieve our mission of enhancing the quality of life and protecting the human rights of people in our community—all people in our community.

It's About Policing with the Soul

Soulful policing requires putting on your intellectual cap and applying your sociological imagination to get to know the community from personal experiences that build genuine rapport with members of the community. The ability to see the world through the eyes of those you police, protect, and serve will allow you to become a better police officer, and further, a better ambassador to your profession. What's more, such deep understanding and insight into the hearts and soul of the community may enrich your life and make you a better person. It's about policing with the soul, a necessary step toward human rights policing.

Reimaging Policing into the Future

While we have focused on human rights policing in our current historical moment and provided the path forward to make human rights policing a possibility today, we believe that the future will require the structural change of policing as an institution.

The main function of law enforcement today is to help uphold class inequality. Police, often unknowingly, mainly exist to protect the class positions of the opulent against the masses. In short, they perform the dirty work of the rich to keep the "rabble" in check. As discussed throughout this book, police "police" crimes of the poor while largely ignoring crimes of the rich and powerful. While we believe that police must uphold the human rights of everyone, including all people who become victims of any human rights violation, from theft to robbery, or any act of violence, we also believe that police should uphold human rights by investigating the offenses of perpetrators and holding them, regardless of their class position, accountable. Law enforcement will remain necessary in policing, and will involve temporarily restricting a perpetrator's (burglar, thief, armed robber) human rights, but a focus on protecting and enforcing human rights should become the main function of policing. We must always keep in mind that both the human rights of victims and perpetrators must be kept into account and a remain focal point of law enforcement.

In an age of unprecedented class inequalities and heightened relative deprivation, people begin to experience an acute sense of social injustice that raises their feelings of discontent to levels that threaten to give rise to crime, social upheaval, civil disobedience, mass resistance, collective action, protest, transgression, disorder, and acts of revolution. In our current historical trajectory, police officers will be stuck in the middle of the tensions between the elite and the masses.

And it will not end well.

The time will come for police officers, law enforcement agents, and criminal justice professionals to decide whose side are they on. Will the police become the enforcers of the status quo or the protectors of the people's human rights?

For now, it's time to focus away from arresting people and instead concentrate on protecting their human rights against the global parasites that seek to prevent people from enjoying their human rights for class interests and personal gain.

It's time to reimagine policing.

We believe that the future of policing needs to focus almost exclusively on protecting the human rights of all people police officers "protect and serve." What's more, the moto of every police department should be "to protect and serve the human rights of the people." This means that police officers should transition out of arresting and incarcerating humans in cages and instead focus on protecting the human rights of community members, especially the most institutionally vulnerable, and further, helping provide them with resources that allow people to enjoy all the human rights that belong to them.

We reimagine the function of law enforcement as an institution that exists to protect the human rights, defined in the United Nations Declaration of Human Rights and its 30 articles, of all people against those that seek to prevent people from enjoying their human rights.

This entails protecting the human rights of the people against those that prevent others from enjoying their rights.

For example, instead of arresting or ticketing homeless people for loitering, panhandling, and vagrancy, or removing homeless camps out of urban areas, police officers can protect the human rights of the people living in homeless conditions. Further, police can serve as liaisons for the homeless community, providing them with resources to find acceptable housing, or at least access to people and organizations set up to find housing for everyone who needs it. In the wealthiest countries on Earth, homelessness is an unforgivable sin and violation of human rights. These populations deserve, like everyone else, to enjoy their natural human rights, and police can lead the way.

For another example, school resource police officers should serve the role of protecting students of human rights violations and, further, serve as positive role models for students while providing them every resource possible to meet their challenges. Arrest and incarceration should only happen in the most egregious of situations, such as murder or extreme acts of violence.

Take another example. Instead of targeting the poor and marginalized for petty crimes, police can patrol poor communities, making sure community members have the opportunity to enjoy their human rights, for example seek proper healthcare, safety, healthy food, proper drinking water, and other types of basic resources most people take for granted. Imagine police officers patrolling their sections investigating human rights concerns of community members. In other words, police should serve communities by making sure everyone has the opportunity to enjoy their human rights, and that the human rights of community members are not being violated. The police can serve as the liaison between community members and organizations that provide resources to people.

In essence, we believe that the main function of policing should transition to protecting the human rights of all people in the community. Instead of focusing on arresting people or handing out tickets and citations, police should devote their resources to patrolling communities and engaging in a type of community policing that enforces and protects human rights. Arrest and incarceration should only happen in the most egregious of situations, and such arrests should only last until the person no longer poses a threat to other community members.

But most important, the community should dictate to law enforcement exactly how they want to be policed, never the other way around.

As we continue to experience rapid social transformation, and as we push toward a new era in human history, it's time to reimagine the world we want to become. It's time to reimagine all of our political, social, and economic institutions. It's time to make human rights the primary focus in our new institutional arrangements of society. It's time to reimagine policing into an institution that focuses primarily on serving and protecting the human rights of all people. It starts with police, the unexpected potential harbingers of human rights, and it spreads to every institution leading to a society where all people enjoy the human rights that naturally belong to us all.

Suggested Videos and Activities

Interview with a Community Organization on Human Rights Policing

Instructions: This assignment has two parts. Part one asks you to watch the documentary *13th*. Part two asks you to interview members of a community organization on their perspectives of human rights and policing. Details follow below.

Activity One: 13th

> Neither slavery nor involuntary servitude, except as a punishment for crime whereof the party shall have been duly convicted, shall exist within the United States, or any place subject to their jurisdiction.
>
> (13th Amendment of the United States Constitution)

Please watch the documentary *13th* that analyzes United States Criminal Justice System, perhaps with some friends, family, or colleagues. Prior to talking with the community group, we ask you to watch the documentary *13th* (see the link in next section), analyzing the United States Criminal Justice System. The purpose of watching this film is to understand the current critiques against the criminal justice system, of which police are a part, and the structural problems associated with it. The documentary offers views about the entire criminal justice system that members of your community might share. For this reason, we want to be aware of current critiques against the criminal justice system before interviewing members of the community.

The documentary analyzes race, justice, and mass incarceration, contending that the United States criminalized black people with a manufactured "war on drugs," racist laws, and a racist criminal justice system. Political ideologies (Clinton's "super-predator," etc.), media fabrications, and manufactured moral panics, they argue, created unrealistic fears of minorities, especially young black men as folk devils, pariahs, and criminals used to justify the brutal imprisonment and continued enslavement of black people—to this day. Meanwhile, this prison industrial complex that cages 25 percent of the world's prisoners (the US has 5 percent of the world's population) produces a billion-dollar business that enriches our most powerful corporations. Corporate owners, it is argued, still reap the benefit of profits from slavery. In the end, the film *13th* argues that slavery, segregation, and systemic oppression continues through a system of mass incarceration, the war on drugs, the criminal justice system (policies, laws and sentencing procedures), political ideology, and media-created fictions that depict minority people with negative images.

You can gain access to the film using the link below:
https://topdocumentaryfilms.com/13th/

Activity Two: Interviewing a Community Organization

Interview members of a community organization (e.g., university student or professor organization, Black Lives Matter, religious groups or leaders, grassroots organizers, high school student organization, YWCA, and/or other community organizations) on their perspectives of how police officers can apply human rights to their community. Find out how they perceive the best practices for police officers to respect and ensure that community members enjoy the human rights that belong to them. If possible, try to find a community group or organization that has been vocal (even critical) about police practices. The purpose of this assignment is to understand human rights from the points of view of community members.

In this activity, please discuss your findings from this interview and provide some thoughts for reflection on how this might inform your police work, specifically related to applying human rights to policing. What is the major takeaway from your discussion with the community organization, and how can this be used to achieve our goals for human rights policing?

Here are some suggestions and guidelines for talking with members of a community organization about their perspectives of what human rights policing should look like, or include, in their community. Since our task is to learn from them, it's important to keep the conversations with community members comfortable, friendly, casual, and informal.

Just a suggestion, but we recommend for you to define human rights for community members as, "Human rights are those that belong to all human beings and to which all humans are entitled without discrimination, regardless of sex, nationality, ethnicity, language, religion, citizenship or any other status."

Further, consider providing some examples such as:

- "right to life and liberty
- freedom from slavery and torture
- freedom of opinion and expression
- right to work and education, etc.
- … and many more"

Perhaps also consider adding, "Human rights policing means that police allow people to enjoy all the rights that belong to them, to the extent possible, while also protecting and serving the community."

Finally, and importantly, you might also want to ask the following questions:

"What would human rights policing look like to you?"

"What else can police do to help implement human rights policing in your community?"

Notes

1 Kerouac, Jack. 1997. *On the Road*. New York: Viking.
2 Dickinson, Emily, and R. W. Franklin. 1999. *The Poems of Emily Dickinson*. Reading ed. Cambridge, MA: Belknap Press.
3 Emerson, Ralph Waldo, and Edward L. Ericson. 1986. *Emerson on Transcendentalism*. New York: Ungar.
4 Melville, Herman, and Tony Tanner. 1998. *Moby Dick*. Oxford: Oxford University Press.
5 Gilman, Charlotte Perkins, and Lynne Sharon Schwartz. 1989. *The Yellow Wallpaper and Other Writings*. New York: Bantam Books.
6 Hawthorne, Nathaniel, and Nathaniel Hawthorne. 1996. *Young Goodman Brown*. Charlottesville, VA: University of Virginia Library.
7 Karmel, Pepe, and N. Y. York. 1999. *Jackson Pollock: Interviews, Articles, and Reviews*. New York: Museum of Modern Art.
8 Holmes, Linda Janet. *Savoring the Salt: The Legacy of Toni Cade Bambara*. Philadelphia: Temple University Press, 2007. "The Lesson" is a story about a well-intentioned schoolteacher sending her poor black students from Harlem to Manhattan's expensive FAO Schwartz toy store. The students are exposed to the world outside of their oppressed community, and in the process of this contradiction find tragic enlightenment bringing them to the window if what can be argues as *it*—ushering a moment of crisis in the underlying reality of the social world.
9 Doyno, Victor. 1991. *Writing Huck Finn: Mark Twain's Creative Process*. Philadelphia: University of Pennsylvania Press.
10 Mellow, James R. 1992. *Hemingway: A Life without Consequences*. Boston: Houghton Mifflin.
11 This is an unpublished 1920s quote recorded by Howard Becker.
12 Marx states: "Religious distress is at the same time the expression of real distress and the protest against real distress. Religion is the sigh of the oppressed creature, the heart of a heartless world, just as it is the spirit of a spiritless situation. It is the opium of the people" (*Critique of Hegel's Philosophy of Right*).

References

Marina, Peter. 2013. *Getting the Holy Ghost: Urban Ethnography in a Brooklyn Pentecostal Tongue-speaking Church*. Lanham, MD: Lexington Books.
Marina, Peter. 2017. *Down and Out in New Orleans: Transgressive Living in the Informal Economy*. New York: Columbia University Press.
MacLean, Annie Marion. 1899. "Two Weeks in a Department Store." *American Journal of Sociology* 4: 721–741.
MacLean, Annie Marion. 1903. "The Sweatshop in Summer." *American Journal of Sociology* 9: 289–309.
Mooney, Jane. 2020. *The Theoretical Foundations of Criminology: Place, Time and Context*. Oxford, UK: Routledge Press.

Chapter 6

Policy Suggestions, Human Rights, and the Future of Policing

Introduction

We end the book with a brief review of the chapters, a brief discussion on kindness and human rights, some thoughts on other threats to human rights policing, the future of policing in the United States and beyond, and the implications for human rights policing as we advance into an uncertain future. The chapter summaries show how each chapter served as part of the process of understanding human rights and how to apply them throughout one's career as a police officers and criminal justice professional. We discuss what lies ahead for the future of policing and the important role of human rights in that future. We also discuss how police officers can be the arbiters of change focusing on the importance of putting human rights "front-and-center" in law enforcement. We stress that human rights policing can serve both the police and their communities well. In the end, human rights policing can make practical change today and help police officers and their departments transition through the changes in policing that will inevitably occur in the future. We believe that human rights policing can become an established model for law enforcement as we push toward this late stage of modernity.

Brief Chapter Summaries

Chapter 1: Human Rights Policing, introduces readers to human rights policing, arguing for human rights in extraordinary times, discussing the goals for human rights policing, sharing thoughts on 30 years of policing, and offering some important points of departure for the book. At the end of the chapter, we asked readers how they would define human rights, how important they are to policing today, and if they have ever thought about applying human rights to their everyday police work. We want to know if the reader believes in the value of applying human rights policing to the field of law enforcement.

Chapter 2: Connecting Human Rights to Policing, calls on police officers to unite under the concept of human rights policing while discussing the meaning and evolution of human rights, the United Nations Declaration of Human Rights, the International Covenant on Civil and Political Rights, and finally human rights from the perspectives of various police officers. In the end, Chapter 2 asks readers to apply what they learned in the chapter to give examples of the three types of police social interactions. Further, we ask readers to discuss three human rights they find most important to policing, their interpretation of those rights, and why they find them most important to policing.

Chapter 3: Police, Power, Agency, and Human Rights, questions who watches the watchman. The chapter covers the definition and meaning of power, the origin of power, and the great philosophical debate between human agency and determinism. The chapter continues with an in-depth discussion on the meaning and potential for human agency and, more importantly,

DOI: 10.4324/9781003220282-7

applying human agency to human rights policing. The chapter also discusses threats to the application of human rights, covering moral panics and the manufacturing of folk devils using an example from the British television show *Black Mirror*. The chapter asks the reader, "What do you see? … How will you, as a police officer, treat the individual: as a folk devil or a human being deserving of their rights?" In the end, we ask readers to apply what they learned from the chapter to discuss if they believe in the potential for human agency, how they apply their human agency to police work, the importance for human agency to achieve the goals of human rights policing, and how to police those deemed folk devils.

Chapter 4: The Sociological Imagination and Human Rights Policing, introduces the sociological imagination as a tool for understanding people and the world they inhabit. We offer a brief discussion on the meaning of the sociological imagination and how to use it when looking at people and their community. Since we, as authors, serve the discipline of criminology, we offer examples from criminology to discuss how to use the sociological imagination to understand the world beyond the subjective experiences of our own lives. The chapter strives to impart the sociological imagination to readers so they can use it to better understand their communities and, further, to better protect and serve them while conducting police work. We continued with a discussion on the relationship between storytelling and human rights. People have the right to tell their own stories, but oftentimes academics, journalists, and various media platforms strip people of their voice and right to self-representation, and this often leads to the double consciousness and feelings of twoness—making other people outsiders, inferiors, and "others." In the end, we ask you to apply the lessons learned in this chapter on the sociological imagination to a member of the community with whom you experienced a negative interaction, or with someone you have arrested, to tell the community member's story and life circumstances.

Chapter 5: Engaging with the Community on Human Rights, introduces the reader to what we call a soulful policing that asks police officers to use some of the ideas from this book to consider how people in their community make sense of their world and, further, draw meaning from it. To understand the world, or the community one protects and serves, it becomes important to get the seat of one's pants dirty—Chicago School style—and venture into community spaces where people live out their biographies and give meaning to their world. Police officers are asked to temporarily trade their police lenses with a sociological lens to see the connection between structural issues and personal troubles to understand the people in their community as well as use *verstehen* (or the ability to see the world from the actor's point of view) to see how people make meaning in the community spaces they inhabit. The authors provide stories to show how we can learn about what makes people tick when we go into the community to learn about social life from first-hand observations and experiences. In these examples, we learn about Pentecostal tongue speakers in an Afro-Caribbean community in Brooklyn, social life in down and out New Orleans, and the French Quarter LGBTQ+ community. In the end, police officers can learn more about their community from the perspectives of those they police, protect, and serve.

Chapter 6: Applying Human Rights Policing discusses kindness, the blasé attitude and, further, provides general national policy recommendations and policy recommendations for policing as we reimagine law enforcement in the 21st century. We conclude with some final thoughts on the future of policing in the United States and beyond, and the implications for human rights policing as we advance into an uncertain future.

On Kindness

kind (adj.)

"Friendly, deliberately doing good to others," Middle English …, "benign, compassionate, loving, full of tenderness" (c. 1300).

To police, being a good cop means following the law. To community members, good cops treat people with dignity and respect—in short, kindness.

While both remain important, both meanings of "good" cops fall well short of the goals of human rights policing.

Kindness, while important, is a necessary but insufficient condition for human rights policing.

It's important to clarify this difference between applying human rights and applying kindness to one's actions toward others. People, we argue, would much prefer to enjoy their human rights than receive kindness from people who violate their human rights. I'm sure some kind people in the military industrial complex order bombs to be dropped in Somalia, killing dozens of innocent people in one of the poorest countries on earth. Perhaps some people prefer kind, decent diversity bombs dropping on their villages killing their children and families. But perhaps not. I believe most people would rather rude people letting them live rather than kinder people dropping bombs on them.

Perhaps some extreme examples will best demonstrate the difference between applying human rights and applying kindness to our actions toward others. To further understand this concept, it's important to discuss the problem of collapsing the individual with the institution.

Many people assume that if an institution is evil, or severely flawed, all the individuals who belong to that institution are equally evil or flawed. For example, one might think that the atomic bomb is evil, but that does not mean everyone who produced the atomic bomb is equally evil.

A Jewish scholar and personal friend provided me with a rather powerful, even if uncomfortable, example to illustrate the point of collapsing the individual with the institution. He explains that there were certain members of the Nazi regime in Germany that were "nicer" than other Nazis while carrying out their evil duties against the Jewish and Roma people, among others.

Relatedly, some white slave owners were "kinder" to their slaves than others while engaging in the evils of slavery. But regardless of their degree of "kindness," I'm sure both groups would have preferred to enjoy their human rights, that is, to not get gassed, whipped, and enslaved.

Hannah Arendt's (1963) concept of the banality of evil suggests that people, who are not necessarily evil, commit evil acts while dutifully obeying bureaucratic orders. After watching Adolf Eichmann's trail for his participation in the Nazi holocaust, Arendt observed:

> I was struck by the manifest shallowness in the doer that made it impossible to trace the uncontestable evil of his deeds to any deeper level of roots or motives. The deeds were monstrous, but the doer—at least the very effective one now on trial—was quite ordinary, commonplace, and neither demonic nor monstrous.
>
> (Arendt 1978, 3)

In other words, non-evil people can do evil in the performance of their job duties. "Normal" people, like some argued of Eichmann, were able to commit evil acts simply following laws, fulfilling bureaucratic duties, and advancing one's career. While most people, to some extent, fulfill Ward Churchill's (2003) concept of "little Eichmanns" in their complicity to the horrors around us, these people are not all equally evil in their participation in a society that produces evil. In short, in an evil society or an evil institution, not all people are equally evil monsters.

Similarly, while both the holocaust and the institution of slavery exemplify pure evil, not everyone who took part in those institutions was equally evil. Similarly, while some people condemn the criminal justice system and the institution of law enforcement, and perhaps for good reason, it's important not to assume every police officer and criminal justice professional is that institution. People interacting with police officers would most certainly prefer a rude cop allowing them to enjoy their human rights rather than a kind cop preventing them from enjoying their human rights.

A student once argued that our exposure to violence leads to increased violence in society. I, in turn, mentioned that perhaps our lack of exposure to violence leads to increased violence. If we could see the actual impact of American bombs dropping on civilian targets in the Middle East, with horrible images of a barely alive baby crawling to its dead mother's corpse to breastfeed or terrified prisoners in the many black sites of the United States government, many people would draw pause on violating the human rights of complete strangers across the world who pose no threat to the Western world.

As stressed throughout this book, being a decent, kind person is important to life, and important to policing, but it falls short of implementing human rights. Applying human rights requires using agency, going beyond our social expectations to act in ways we would otherwise never consider. Using agency allows people the possibility to act in transcendent and extraordinary ways, like using power for someone else's benefit. When police officers act in extraordinary ways, they can become human rights protectors ensuring that people enjoy, to the greatest degree possible, all of the human rights that belong to them. Human rights policing requires that police officers use their agency to find creative ways that allow people to enjoy those rights listed in the Declaration of Human Rights, among others, even in the most difficult of circumstances.

But what about rights? Looking at many other countries around the world, the prospects of human rights look rather dismal. Even basic observations from the US, the UK, and other Western European domestic and international policies reveal a picture on human rights that does not look much better than other countries often labeled as lacking in human rights. For example, the United States inhumanly imprisons, and even tortures, thousands of migrants before deporting them back to countries that American political and economic policies devastated.[1] The United States incarcerates far more people than any other country on the planet, often for non-violent offenses and a manufactured war on drugs. In a rare moment of honesty, when presented the question if international policy that resulted in killing half a million children in Iraq to advance American interest was worth the price, Madeleine Albright stated that yes, it was worth the price.[2]

In other words, human rights exist in theory, not practice, in the United States, the United Kingdom, and the world. The United States is no exception to the cruelty we see other terrorists, dictators, and other nation-states commit in the world to advance their own interests. We engage in constant wars killing millions of people to support an economic system that bulldozes anything and everything it its path. We engage in global economic crimes, like the embargoes against Cuba and Iran, that kill and starve the civilian populations to advance the political and economic interests of the ruling elite. We have one political party with two factions, republicans and democrats, that abandoned the American people and left them to fend for themselves without labor unions, health care, worker's rights, and social safety nets while the people must deal with massive inflation, disappearing pensions, worker insecurity, and absurd higher costs of living. In short, what human rights really exist for most people, including the so-called developed, industrialized world? For most people on the planet, especially for those whose income drops below a certain level (near, at, or below poverty), human rights don't exist, no matter how nice and decent some people act toward them.

But we must ask how can we make applying human rights a reality, into tangible actions. It's a good question because *how* has never been done before. All we have is *what*. We know what human rights are, and we, as a civilization, wrote them down in fancy documents.

But we have not answered how.

But we're trying, which is the point of this book. Human rights policing paves the way for actual, tangible steps to create a world in which human rights become the highest principle, and practice, of the land. Of course, as stressed throughout this book, realizing human agency becomes critical to implement human rights.

Can you use your agency to apply human rights to people, including the worst of them? We, as a people, drop bombs on strangers and buy clothes from companies that enslave children. It's easy to violate people's human rights; it comes almost naturally. Put differently, it's too easy to violate people's rights, and we, as a people, do it for breakfast, lunch, dinner, and one more time before bed. It's time to stop this practice. And we believe police can do it; police can be the world leaders in making human rights a reality in society. That requires agency.

We discussed the power of the sociological imagination and *verstehen* to see the world beyond the limited private orbit of your own life. We use this way of thinking to not only understand and interpret this world with powerful new insights, but also with our ability to interpret the world from the actor's point of view. We learned how easy it is to "other" people, to make them feel this two-ness and double consciousness. It's been done to us. And we do it to others, all the time. We do it from the time we get up in the morning until we go to bed. We do it without thinking about it. Now we ask the reader to think about it, use your agency, use *verstehen* and the sociological imagination to make people feel one-ness and belonging. This happens when we empower people, and people find better access to power when in full enjoyment of human rights.

It's also essential to empower the voices of community members who tell us their perspective of what human rights policing looks like, giving us important insight into finding new ways to incorporate the practice into policing behavior. Perhaps police can be the harbingers of a new era where human rights become more than a document or concept, but a real practice. We need the voice of community members. We also need soulful policing.

Nice and polite is insufficient for human rights policing. It doesn't cut it for police officers or criminal justice professionals. What matters most is the application of human rights into all of our interactions with other people, beyond politeness and kindness.

We hope the reader will constantly think about how to apply human rights to their jobs, and life, to help make it a reality. We, the authors, will always think about how to apply human rights to our lives in all our encounters with others, and all of our decision making (I've even radically changed my consumption behavior to not buy anything that exploits people, earth, and animals) because if we don't change, if we don't apply human rights in our actions as a species, our future is not very bright. But we believe in agency. We believe in the people. We believe in our reader. We believe that police officers, law enforcement agents, and criminal justice professionals can become the arbiters of human rights and lead the way toward a brighter future. We will change the direction of history if we apply human rights to our actions. It's the only way to avoid falling into the eternal goodnight as a species.

But threats to human rights policing always remain lurking at bay.

The Blasé Attitude and Human Rights Policing

In his brilliant essay "Metropolis and Mental Life" classical sociologist Georg Simmel (1903) discusses how urban dwellers of the great metropolis subconsciously develop a protective organ, or an internal subconscious self-defense mechanism, to defend themselves against the massive onslaught of external stimuli they encounter living in the city. He argues that the psychology of the modern urban dweller must confront the "intensification of emotional life due to the swift and continuous shift of external and internal stimuli" one faces in city life. Urbanites subconsciously protect their psychological state of being under constant threat of attack from the "profound disruption" as well as the constant "fluctuations and discontinu-ities" that derive from the external milieu of the city. As a result of this protective organ that shields the metropolitan type from the onslaught of "rapidly shifting stimulations," the city dweller develops a blasé attitude, or an attitude of indifference, toward people and events. This type of intellectualistic quality protects one's inner life against the power of the metropolis to dominate the self (Ibid).

As a result of this protective organ, an intellectualistic quality develops within the mental life of urban dwellers, one that refuses to act on an emotional or empathetic level to the experiences other people encounter in the city. The intensification of this type of mental con-sciousness produces a mental state least sensitive to others, removed from the personality of the urban dweller. In short, the urban inhabitant subconsciously develops a cold, calculating, rationalistic attitude of indifference—a blasé attitude—in the city to protect themselves from the ongoing, constant attack of external stimuli of city life and the, at times, heart-wrenching experiences that so many people face in the social life of the city (Ibid).

Police officers also subconsciously develop this protective organ to protect themselves from all the external stimuli they encounter on the job, events that could be quite troubling to the human psyche. Indeed, police officers see the worst aspects of human life, and often witness traumatic cases of rape, sexual assault, murder, and violence. As a result of this protective organ, police officers themselves often develop the blasé attitude of indifference to the personal tra-gedies people experience.

The newly minted police officer often begins to develop this subconscious self-protective organ early in one's career. In the passage that follows below, the second author reveals how police officers develop this blasé attitude—a process that begins on the first days of the job and advances throughout one's career.

Developing the Blasé Attitude: Notes from the N.O.P.D.

At first, I did not understand it. How could a human being not be moved at the sight of a violent murder? It was such a tragedy.

But to my partner, it just another day. He was not moved.

I was paralyzed at the sight. But now I am getting ahead of myself.

My first homicide scene.

I was just a rookie on my first week out of police academy. On my first day, I got dressed in police attire at home to get ready for the adventure I had dreamed about for a long time. I put on my blue uniform: shirt, dark blue pants and, of course, the best part that I had been waiting for so many weeks at the academy, my gun belt. I put on my police hat, went to the mirror, and felt proud. I was now a real police officer.

So, I got in my car and drove to the Second District Police Station. Having graduated at the top of my class, I was given any district assignment I wanted. I chose the second district because it had everything: the Tulane University section, the River Bend area with so many businesses and boutiques, and, above all, some high crime areas. The area was popping.

I arrived at the district station and met with the welcoming lieutenant. He told me that I would be assigned to ride with an experienced officer who would show me the ropes. I sat for roll call, listening to the different crimes from the previous day as well as the subjects wanted for the alleged crimes. Then the best part, my new partner came to me, introduced himself, and said, "Son, forget what they taught you at the academy, I will teach you real police work." Well, I won't bore you with the first two days. Sure, we responded to a few burglaries, armed robberies, and purse-snatching calls, all on a code two, complete with siren and lights.

Oh yes, I was the real police.

The third day was different.

At about an hour after roll call, a radio dispatch was broadcast for all district units to respond to a signal 34—a shooting in progress. My partner looked at me, stating, "Son, you are in for it. Tell the dispatcher that we are responding and get a description." I got on the air to advise the dispatcher. With lights and siren, we were speeding to the intersection in question. As we were a few blocks away, my partner turned off the siren, ordering, "Listen." I heard gunfire, about ten shots.

My heart was speeding faster than the police car.

We arrived, guns in hand, on the scene and advised the dispatcher of our arrival while looking around. There was a man laying down on the sidewalk right at the corner. There was blood everywhere. There were also a bunch of empty casings from a semi-automatic weapon. I looked at the man, and seeing that he was still alive, I went to him, knelt down, raised his head with my hand, and asked him who had done this to him.

I'll never forget how he responded.

He said, "Don't worry about it, I'll get him myself." I tried to plead with him to tell me what happened, but he couldn't.

He died as I was holding his head.

I got up, looked at my hands full of blood, and walked around in a daze, unable to assimilate what I had just experienced. Then, I realized that my partner was screaming at me to get a hold of myself and advise the dispatcher to send EMS to confirm we had a homicide. I followed my partner, setting up a perimeter to protect the scene and to try to locate witnesses. Of course, there was nobody around. We stayed on the scene for about half an hour until the Homicide Unit relieved us. Actually, the platoon sergeant told us to clear the scene to remain available for the next code two (emergency call with priority).

As we got back in the car, my partner looked at me, smiling, and then said: "Pedro, you did good. You want to get something to eat?"

I told him that right about now I could not eat. I needed some time to get over that last experience. My partner understood. He told me that he had a similar reaction when he first came on the job. But now, he said, he didn't let those experiences bother him.

I went home that night but could not sleep. I had that image in my mind. I could see this poor man as he was going through the process of dying. I went through it in my mind over and over and what I saw the moment he died was his soul, or something actually rising above his body, only to disappear. The body was left behind motionless and lifeless. It was many years later that I could actually tell my friends and my son about this experience. I was truly traumatized.

Over time, I continued to respond to many calls for service where there was much suffering. There were traffic accidents involving fatalities, family disturbances where women and children were badly hurt, child abuse, rapes, suicides, and many other tragic situations. What I noticed was that as time passed, I was more immune to the suffering. Not that I did not have empathy for those who suffered, I certainly did. But with time, I was not as affected and could quickly forget and go to the next call. I noticed the same reactions from my fellow officers. They cared about the people, but could shake off the tragedies other people experiences. Without knowing it, we eventually learned how to put each tragedy behind us and move on to the next call. There was really no other way to cope with this job and survive.

We became blasé.

The future of human rights policing depends, in part, on police officers and criminal justice professionals resisting the tendency to become blasé when protecting and serving the people in our communities—one of the most trusted positions in society. If we want to maintain our integrity and worthiness of this position of trust, and if we want to make human rights policing a reality, we must refuse to become blasé.

Solutions to the Blasé Attitude in Law Enforcement and Criminal Justice System: When the blasé attitude affects first responders, especially police and those who work in the criminal justice system, the condition can have grave consequences for the people in the community. We offer a brief practical solution and a more personal solution to help ameliorate the problem of the blasé.

On a practical level, police agencies need to address the blasé attitude through in-service training at least twice a year. The training should include an awareness of the blasé condition that happens when police respond and handle situations with people who have experienced trauma. Victims of incidents such as robberies, family disturbances, rapes, traffic accidents involving injuries, suicides, medical emergencies, and homicides should be considered. The training should also include police exposure to friends and relatives of those people who have experienced such trauma and how that trauma and the police handling of it has affected them. Psychologists and sociologists should be part of that training as well.

On a personal level, once aware of the existence of the blasé attitude, especially from those who experience so much external stimuli and human trauma, it becomes a choice law enforcement and criminal justice professionals make on a daily basis. While the universe as a whole is indifferent to an individual's pain and suffering, to that individual, that pain and suffering is unique and intense, it's the entire world—it's everything. Even when it means little to us, we must remember that the person is feeling and experiencing a unique situation that causes them fear, suffering, and pain, just like we would experience if the situation were reversed. Police officers and criminal justice professionals must remain constantly cognizant of the blasé attitude always lurking at bay, and do everything in their power to resist it.

Policy Suggestions

We believe that the policy changes recommended below will help reduce street crime in society and improve policing, and in particular, advance the goals of human rights policing. We discuss general policy changes at the national level as well as specific policy changes for policing in the United States and beyond. While political and economic elites on both sides of the political spectrum will resist the policy changes recommended below, we believe grassroots organizing and intense public pressure on elected officials could make our policy recommendations possible. We believe that fighting for such changes will improve society as a whole, reduce street crime, and improve policing as we reimagine law enforcement in the 21st century.

General Policy Changes at the National Level

- End Forever Wars and International Military Bases
- End Mass Violence Against the Earth and Non-Human Animals
- End the War on Drugs and Decriminalize all Drugs
- End For-Profit Prisons
- Abolish the Prison-Industrial Complex
- Abolish the Death Penalty
- Universal Healthcare/Medicare-for-All
- End Homelessness (Homelessness + Vacant Houses = Society fails)
- $20 Dollar Minimum Wage

- End Welfare for the Rich Programs & Tax the Rich
- End Citizens United and Corporate Lobbying
- End Corporate Influence on Social Policy
- National Support for Labor Unions
- Create a Third Major Party

We address each policy suggestion below. While disagreement will surely exist with each of these policy suggestions, we believe a larger dialogue allows us to reach shared common goals, beyond our relatively minor political disagreement, that will culminate in a call for action to make historical change for the benefit of the human species.

One: End Forever Wars and International Military Bases

The United States Congress, in a bipartisan decision during a global pandemic, recently passed the 778 billion National Defense Authorization Act (37 billion more than the previous budget, or just over three-quarters of a trillion dollars), to continue its global violence and wars of empire (Johnson 2021).[3] Instead of funding social programs to improve education, climate, healthcare, mental health, homelessness, drug addiction, policing, and other social programs to improve the lives of Americans and serve the needs of people, the United States government decided to continue its war-profiteering ways. United States tax dollars also fund about 750 military bases in at least 80 countries around the world and send special operations commandos to 154 countries (Hussein and Hadded 2021).[4] Perhaps it was the decorated marine and two-time Medal of Honor recipient Smedley Butler who said it best on the truth about war in his 1935 book *War is a Racket*:

> War is a racket. It always has been. It is possibly the oldest, easily the most profitable, surely the most vicious. It is the only one international in scope. It is the only one in which the profits are reckoned in dollars and the losses in lives. A racket is best described, I believe, as something that is not what it seems to the majority of the people. Only a small "inside" group knows what it is about. It is conducted for the benefit of the very few, at the expense of the very many. Out of war a few people make huge fortunes.
>
> (Butler 2018)

Our policy recommendation on giving our hard-earned tax dollars to the military industrial complex and its global wars is the same recommendation the great Smedley Butler provided almost a century ago:

> Three steps must be taken to smash the war racket. We must take the profit out of war. We must permit the youth of the land who would bear arms to decide whether or not there should be war. We must limit our military forces to home defense purposes.

Most Americans, we believe, would prefer to use their tax dollars on social programs that improve the lives of the people, not on the few politicians, war contactors, weapons manufacturers, and war mongering corporate lobbyists who profit from war and death.

What's more, if we don't want a violent society, perhaps we shouldn't have a violent government. If example serves as the best characteristic of a leader, then our political and economic "leaders" should lead the way toward non-violence. As Chomsky states, "Everyone's worried about stopping terrorism. Well, there's a really easy way: Stop participating in it." Similarly, if we want to reduce violence in our city streets from people on both sides of the law, then our "leaders" should stop serving as the quintessential example of violence in society. In other words, if we want to end violence, we as a country must stop participating in it.

On the *Damned Human Race*, Mark Twain states:

> Man is the only animal that deals in that atrocity of atrocities, War. He is the only one that gathers his brethren about him and goes forth in cold blood and with calm pulse to exterminate his kind. He is the only animal that for sordid wages will march out, as the Hessians did in our Revolution, and as the boyish Prince Napoleon did in the Zulu war, and help to slaughter strangers of his own species who have done him no harm and with whom he has no quarrel.[5]

Perhaps we should refrain from slaughtering our own species. Perhaps war-like societies produce war-like people.

Two: End Mass Violence Against the Earth and Non-Human Animals

Aside from slaughtering our own species, it's well beyond time to reconsider the mass slaughtering of the earth and its non-human animals.

According to the World Wildlife Fund (WWF):

> Humans have only been around for 200,000 years, a tiny blip in the 4.5 billion years of our planet's history. Yet we have had a greater impact on the Earth than any other species. All over the world, we are cutting down forests, using too much water from rivers, choking our oceans with plastic and pushing many animals to extinction. For both people and wildlife to thrive, now and in the future, we need a healthy planet, with a rich variety of plants and animals and vibrant ecosystems.
>
> (WWF 2018)[6]

A recent announcement, from the World Wildlife Fund's 2018 Living Planet Report shows that in the past 40 years human behavior has wiped out a whopping 60 percent of the global wildlife population (Ibid). This loss of animal life, they rightfully argue, poses a threat to human civilization. Further, besides the massive violence practiced against animals in human society—from the meat and dairy industry to deforestation and over-development (among other things)—the global impact of climate change threatens to cause an unprecedented violence to millions of humans. A society violent to its own planet, and destructive of other species on the planet, is also likely to turn its violence against itself. People who grant no mercy to others live without honor, or mercy. If we want healthy, less violent people, perhaps we need a healthy planet—including its plants and animals.

Three: End the War on Drugs and Decriminalize all Drugs

The war on drugs is a complete failure. It does almost nothing to reduce drug use in society but does everything to destroy the lives of millions of people separated from their family and friends while languishing in cages. The war on drugs is another racket that benefits the few in a profitable prison-industrial complex. As Nixon's advisor John Ehrlichman said on the war on drugs:

> You want to know what this was really all about? The Nixon campaign in 1968, and the Nixon White House after that, had two enemies: the antiwar left and black people. … We

knew we couldn't make it illegal to be either against the war or black, but by getting the public to associate the hippies with marijuana and blacks with heroin, and then criminalizing both heavily, we could disrupt those communities. We could arrest their leaders, raid their homes, break up their meetings, and vilify them night after night on the evening news. Did we know we were lying about the drugs? Of course we did.[7]

The war on drugs does not keep people safer, does not curtail drug use and abuse in society, destroys millions of American lives, shoves non-violent people in prison, and puts police in an impossible and dangerous battle that will never succeed. In short, we must end the war on drugs, legalize marijuana and magic mushrooms, decriminalize all drugs, and make drug addiction a mental health issue.

Four: End For-Profit Prisons

Public institutions should remain just that—public. We need to take back control of our social institutions from the hands of corporate oligarchy. Corporations should play no role in our criminal justice system and our prison-industrial complex. In short, take all profit out of prisons.

Five: Abolish the Prison-Industrial Complex

We need to abolish the prison-industrial complex and reserve incarceration only for people who pose an immediate and violent threat to society. All other offenders of criminal law can make restitution in ways that do not involve entry into the prison-industrial complex. The prison-industrial system is part of an old, archaic, uncivilized, and barbaric oppressive institution that no longer belongs in a society that values human rights. Locking humans in cages is a dated and barbarous act that needs to change as we progress to a more civil society that values, and practices, human rights. If, as Smedley Butler said, taking the profit out of war is the only way to end wars, then we must take the profit out of prison to end the oppressive practice of imprisoning our fellow humans in a vast national infrastructure of human cages.

Six: Abolish the Death Penalty

State-sanctioned killings, or many would say murder, must end. Allowing the state moral and physical authority to carry out murder sends the message that life is not sacred. The ramifications of the death penalty on society includes, among other things, the validation of killing and murder as socially acceptable forms of behavior. The government's right to commit violence, any act of violence, on its people must be severely restricted, if not eliminated.

Seven: Universal Healthcare/Medicare-for-All

Healthcare is a human right. In the richest country in the world that gives 778 billion dollars to a for-profit war industry, universal healthcare is easily affordable. The only reason we do not have universal healthcare, like every other first world country, is because it does not benefit the multi-billion-dollar, for-profit, corporate-owned health care industry. We argue for a universal healthcare and a Medicare-for-all on the basic philosophical principles of the social contract in which human beings agree that, in exchange for accepting the power of government over the individual, governments protect human rights such as healthcare. The social contract also holds that we, as a society based on social solidarity, agree to voluntarily give a little of ourselves for the greater health of our society, especially basic health care for all of our brothers and sisters. We also argue that universal healthcare, heavily subsidized or affordable education, and a high minimum wage would increase security and dignity in society while reducing discontent, thereby significantly reducing street crime. As a result, universal healthcare and Medicare-for-all would benefit all people (except for the rich corporate owners of the health care industry) in society, including the police.

Eight: End Homelessness (Homelessness + Vacant Houses = Society fails)

It would cost about $20 billion to end homelessness in the United States.[8] Given that we pay 778 billion toward the military industrial complex that funds unnecessary wars and military bases across the world, only 2 percent of the military budget could end homelessness. While ending homelessness is an easy social problem to solve, and a human rights issue, it also will make life much easier for police officers.

Nine: $20 Dollar Minimum Wage

We should not pay employee salaries of powerful corporations, like Walmart and many others, that refuse to pay workers a living wage that covers the cost of living. We can help end welfare for the poor if we force big companies to pay their workers a living and respectable wage. If every American receives universal healthcare, highly affordable education, and a relatively high basic income for work, discontent in society would decrease and, as a result, so would crime.

Ten: End Welfare for the Rich Programs and Tax the Rich

As discussed earlier in the book, the Cares Act created the largest upward transfer of wealth in human history. While we may never achieve equality, and while it may not even be desirable, a government that serves corporate interests at the expense of the people is a failed government that exacerbates inequality and heightens discontent in society. If we are to end "free" government handouts, let's start with the real "welfare queens"—the corporate billionaires who receive our money for no work. Further, as discussed earlier in the book, the richest and most powerful members of society do not pay their fair share of taxes. The working and middle classes pay the brunt of taxes, taking on the burden of paying for society. It's time the political and economic elite pay their share of taxes for a society that disproportionately benefits them.

Eleven: End Citizens United and Corporate Lobbying

Citizens United made corporations legal persons and allows corporations to make unlimited financial campaign contributions, giving powerful groups of wealthy elites the ability to control elections. Lobbying legalizes bribery in society. Corporations now, literally, write the bills that legislators pass into law. As a result, many people argue that the United States is more of a corporate oligarchy than a true democracy. Discontent heightens, as does crime, when people feel their elected leaders abandoned them.

Twelve: End Corporate Influence on Social Policy

Similar to the above recommendation, corporations should not have influence over social policy. Powerful corporations unite under groups like the American Legislative Exchange

Council is America (ALEC) to write policies that benefit them into law.[9] For example, groups such as ALEC that helped create the age of mass incarceration served the interests of those corporations that benefitted from caging humans in cells. We, the people, control our institutions, not the corporations.

Thirteen: National Support for Labor Unions

Working republicans and democrats fought hard to secure the rights of working people around the world. Labor unions today serve as another institution that protects the basic human rights of workers in a capitalistic, profit-driven economy. If police can have labor unions, so too can other working members of our community. Labor unions provide dignity and respect for workers, thus reducing discontent that leads to crime. In short, nationally supported labor unions benefit police and the community.

Fourteen: Create a Third Major Party

We have a one-party system composed of two factions, the democrats and republicans, that serve the corporate elite. In short, our two political parties have abandoned the American people. It's time for us to abandon them. We need to create a workers' or people's party to reclaim our institutions and advance the interests of the vast majority of people free from corporate interests, especially on the matters of climate, universal healthcare, justice, poverty, universal education, peace, democracy, homelessness, employment, labor unions, and other pressing issues.

Summary: A healthy society produces safe communities largely free from street crime. Clearly, our society is sick. To restore society to health and ameliorate social problems related to crime, we must resolve the structural inequalities that create relative deprivation, or the subjective sense of arbitrary social injustice and unfairness in society, that heightens feelings of discontent, producing a hostility that can lead to street crime and violence. We can expect street violence to continue so long as the structural conditions remain intact that create relative deprivation and discontent. As cultural criminologist Jock Young argues:

> Discontent is a product of relative, not absolute, deprivation. … Sheer poverty, for example, does not necessarily lead to a subculture of discontent; it may, just as easily, lead to quiescence and fatalism. Discontent occurs when comparisons between comparable groups are made which suggest that unnecessary injustices are occurring. … Exploitative cultures have existed for generations without extinction: it is the perception of injustice—relative deprivation—which counts.
>
> (2011)

Ending the pervasive structural inequalities that cause relative deprivation—the main cause of street crime—requires radical social transformation. Meanwhile, the policy changes suggested above make small but necessary steps to help restore society to health, lessen structural inequalities, reduce feelings of discontent related to relative deprivation, and reduce street crime in society. Universal healthcare, free (tax subsidized) higher education, ending student debt, high minimum wages, supporting labor unions that protect workers, creating a third-party giving political power to working Americans, and shifting the burden on the ultra-rich to pay taxes, among other things, will help lead the way for a better future where practicing human rights becomes a possibility in society.

Policy Changes for Policing

- Increase Funding for the Police
- Higher Standards for Hiring and Promotion
- Community-Directed Policing
- Standard Training in Human Rights
- Civilian Community Oversight Board
- Limit Asset Forfeiture
- End War on Drugs and Decriminalize All Drugs
- Limit "No-Knock" Warrants
- Limit Qualified Immunity
- Eliminate Police from Traffic Enforcement
- Lessen the Burden on Police Officers: Eliminate Non-Criminal Calls for Service
- Demilitarize Most Police
- Significantly Reduce Police from Making Arrests at Schools
- Decriminalize Kids
- Reallocate Resources

We now briefly discuss each policy suggestion mentioned above for reimagining policing in the 21st century. Our policy suggestions intend to bring about a larger discourse that, like our general national policy changes, will allow us to reach common goals for the benefit of the global human community as well as the local communities that impact the individual lives of community members and the police that serve them.

One: Increase Funding for the Police

While we argue for taking much of the burden away from police to solve problems they cannot possibly solve (see below), we argue that we should increase the funding for police to provide them everything needed to carry out community wishes on how they want to be policed. Police officers should receive the support of the community on training programs, education, human rights, and community engagements to help them better protect and serve the community. The problems of police have nothing to do with "too much funding" or "too many police officers." If that were the case, less funding and cops would solve the problems of policing. The problems associated with police, real or perceived, have little to do with over-funding and an abundance of police officers. Rather, taking away the burden from police officers to solve problems that various other professionals can solve and funding police officers in training, education, human rights, and increasing positive community engagement can better help both police officers and the communities they serve.

Two: Higher Standards for Hiring and Promotion

We will keep this policy suggestion open to interpretation so that communities can decide for themselves what standards they expect of their police for hiring and promotion. In general, we suggest that all police officers receive college degrees, some education in the liberal arts and humanities, human rights training, community engagement training, police and firearms training, and other types of professional development to better protect and serve the community.

Three: Community-Directed Policing

Policing should be a collective community endeavor, not a unilateral decision of a police department, or police officers, telling a community how it will be policed. In short, police should not dictate how a community will be policed. Rather, the community should inform law enforcement how it wants to be policed. For example, if the community does not want their kids formally arrested for underage drinking and smoking, and instead wants their children taken to the police station to await their parents, the police should carry out the wants of the community. As another example, if the community does not want people arrested for simple drug possession, the police should follow the dictates of the community. Put simply, the community should dictate how it wants to be policed, not the other way around.

Four: Standard Training in Human Rights

While it might seem self-serving, we will let our readers decide the merit of such claims. We argue that a standard human rights training, such as the one provided in this book, should serve as a national, standard model of policing in society. Human rights policing gives police officers the primary responsibility to ensure all people enjoy the human rights that naturally belong to them while carrying out their duties to protect and serve the community. Human rights policing must go beyond the legal obligation of civil rights, and further, beyond giving community members kindness and respect. Rather, human rights, as articulated in the United Nations Declaration of Human Rights, requires police officers to actively, as much as legally possible to protect and serve the community, allow community members to enjoy all the human rights that belong to them. It requires police officers to use the sociological imagination to understand the world from the point of view of the people they protect and serve. It also requires police officers to engage in the soulful policing of getting to know the community from extensive engagement and involvement with the community. Police must become part of the communities they protect and serve. Instead of this "us against them" mentality, human rights policing enables police officers to see community members as brothers and sisters united in solidarity to make the community better. We believe that the ideas and concepts discussed throughout this book will make human rights policing a reality in society.

Five: Civilian Community Oversight Board

No institution in society can be trusted if it investigates itself for potential wrongdoing. Law enforcement is no exception to this rule. Simply put, every community needs to have a civilian oversite board of non-governmental community members unaffiliated with the police to investigate complaints of police misconduct, including excessive use of force.

Six: Limit Asset Forfeiture

According to the ACLU, asset forfeiture is a

> police abuse of civil asset forfeiture laws (that) has shaken our nation's conscience. Civil forfeiture allows police to seize—and then keep or sell—any property they allege is involved in a crime. Owners need not ever be arrested or convicted of a crime for their cash, cars, or even real estate to be taken away permanently by the government.[10]

Asset forfeiture laws, potentially make profit over crime-fighting the primary motivation of seizing cash and property, and thereby invites corruption in the institution of law enforcement, as it would any other human-created institution. Even in cases where it does not invite corruption, it certainly leads to distrust of law enforcement and, resultingly, police officers. We argue that asset forfeiture should be limited to the excessive cash or property of people convicted of financial, political, and economic crimes, especially the most powerful people in society.

Seven: End War on Drugs and Decriminalize All Drugs

As stated above, the war on drugs and the criminalization of drugs puts police officers in dangerous positions to solve a problem they cannot possibly solve. Further, it puts millions of our brothers and sisters behind bars for non-violent offenses. To repeat, we must end the war on drugs, legalize marijuana and magic mushrooms, decriminalize all drugs, and make drug addiction a mental health issue. This will significantly reduce our prison and jail population, keep police officers and the community safer, and devote resources to actually helping people with drug addiction.

Eight: Limit "No-Knock" Warrants

In short, with the end of the war on drugs and the decriminalization of drugs, there is little need for most "no-knock" warrants that remain dangerous for both police officers and members of the community. "No-knock" warrants should be limited to situations that pose an imminent threat to society: terrorism, mass shootings, murders, to list a few.

Nine: Limit Qualified Immunity

Qualified immunity is a controversial legal doctrine that protects police officers accused of misconduct. While police advocates argue that it protects police officers from frivolous lawsuits, critics say that it shields police officers from liability when they violate people's civil rights.[11] According to NPR, since civil rights complaints must prove an officer violated a "clearly established law," in past court cases, qualified immunity serves as a catch-22 doctrine that protects, or shields, police officers from civil rights violations difficult to prove.[12] As a result, qualified immunity shields officers accused of misconduct such as excessive use of force, brutality, stealing, and unwarranted killings.[13] While we believe that police officers should be protected from frivolous lawsuits, we also argue that police should not have blanket shielding of civil rights violations and misconduct. In short, we need to limit qualified immunity so that police officers receive protection from frivolous lawsuits and unwarranted complaints, while also taking full legal and criminal responsibility for improper conduct and civil rights abuses.

Ten: Eliminate Police from Traffic Enforcement

Traffic stops put police and community members in unnecessary and highly dangerous situations. Police stops also create too many negative public interactions with the police, thus increasing distrust and hostility against the police. Further, there is not much evidence that traffic stops positively impact traffic safety. This is one situation where it would be easy to replace police with another traffic enforcing agency unrelated to criminal law enforcement. For example, another traffic enforcement agency unrelated to criminal law enforcement might serve the community better, especially in residential and school safety zones. While we remain skeptical of recommending traffic cameras, such surveillance measures, while undemocratic, seem safer than police officers enforcing traffic rules.

Eleven: Lessen the Burden on Police Officers: Eliminate Non-Criminal Calls for Service

Our society has grown too dependent on police. The purpose of police is to make our communities safer, not solve everyone's personal problems. We've heard of people calling the police on neighbors for shoveling snow onto their property, teachers calling the police on students smoking cigarettes, and other types of small problems. We believe that police should stick to the problem of crime and work on making their communities safer. In other words, we need to lessen the burden on police officers. Police officers often respond to calls for service unrelated to crime. What's more, police respond to calls for service that various other professionals can better serve, examples like domestic issues, miscellaneous complaints, mental health issues, medical issues, house alarms, traffic accidents, missing juveniles and persons, and so on.

Twelve: Demilitarize Most Police

Police should not be seen as a foreign occupying force on American soil capable of using war-like violence. While police should have equipment that keeps them safe, police officers looking like military forces only furthers the "us against them" mentality from both cops and community members. Only special divisions in the police department should resemble the military, for example those that handle threats of terrorism, active shootings, and hostage situations.

Thirteen: Significantly Reduce Police from Making Arrests at Schools

Many scholars question the role of police in schools and the merits of arresting kids. If we want to make people violent, and if we want to unnecessarily and needlessly create hardened criminals, put kids in a juvenile detention center at a young age. Keep police officers in school serving as positive role models and "old heads" in the community, but make arrests only for the most egregious of offenses, such as school shootings and stabbings. In other words, we need more officer-friendly and positive role models that foster trust with law enforcement, not threats of arrest and enforcement.

Fourteen: Decriminalize Kids

Walking through the retail store Total Wine & More to buy the elixir of the bourgeoise— wine—I, the first author, noticed a sign at check-out stating "Under 30? Please have ID ready … We arrest minors." While a private corporation has no ability to legally arrest minors, I asked a helpless cashier why the store would want to arrest kids and put them in jail for trying a buy booze, a matter of kicks and giggles fairly typical of curious kids in a Protestant country where alcohol is still largely considered a social taboo. Since when did we have a war on youths? While there is a sociological explanation of society's war on kids stemming from the rise of youth resistant subcultures in England and the United States, for example Mods, Teddy Boys, Rastas, Skinheads, Punks, Goths, Rockers, and Hip-Hoppers, among others, the important point is that kids became perceived as a "problem" in society that required social control and police attention (Clarke et al. 1976). The war on kids is another epic failure in American society. It turns many non-violent youths into violent street criminals—and all for nothing. "Back in the day," as they say, police officers used to call the parents when kids were up to mischief, not arrest them, put them in jail, and give them criminal records along with the negative stigma associated with criminality.

Arresting kids should always be of last resort, and only for the most egregious offenses in society. If we ask why kids cause so many problems for adults, we should also ask why adults cause so many problems for kids. If we look hard in the mirror, perhaps we are projecting our own problems on our kids. In short, kids need support, not jails—end the war on kids.

Fifteen: Reallocate Resources

Again, too much burden is put on police. Other professionals can better serve society on various social issues currently placed on law enforcement. Social workers, mental health professionals, and councilors, among others, should receive financial support and resources to answer non-criminally-related calls for service and other social problems police cannot solve, such as underage drinking, truancy, outside drinking, loitering, kids buying cigarettes, loud noise, and other related social problems.

Summary: As we move forward into the precarious future, it's time to rethink who protects and serves the community. Certainly, police play an important role in protecting and serving the community, and will continue to play a large role in the future, but they cannot remain the only people responsible for such tasks. We must learn self-reliance; we must learn how to protect ourselves. As Henry David Thoreau said, "Rather than love, than money, than fame, give me truth." The truth is we, as a society, have grown too dependent on the police. We expect them to solve our problems and blame them for failing to solve problems they cannot possibly solve. Even those that call on defunding the police often want police protection when it fits their interests. We must also protect ourselves. We can protect ourselves with some of the national policy recommendations made above (universal health care, free (subsidized) higher education, high minimum wages, labor unions, and so on), while also creating programs at national and local levels that provide everyone with community support and resources that lessen the conditions of anomie. When people feel connected to their communities and invested in their institutions that provide dignity and respect, they become less likely to engage in street crime. The responsibility of protecting ourselves falls on other community institutions like the family, schools, universities, hospitals, mental health facilities, and recreational and religious institutions, among others. Teachers, professors, family members, social workers, school and community resource officers, councilors, mental health workers, formal and informal community leaders, coaches, and other community member organizers and members of community organizations must also take on the responsibility of protecting and serving the community. While police remain important, they must play a part of a much larger process.

While some police officers and criminal justice professionals may not agree with all of our policing policy recommendations, we can all agree on the end goals of such policies: to build community solidarity, to strengthen police officers in the community, to make our communities safer, and to spread the responsibility of protecting and serving the community to the people—in solidarity.

Final Thoughts and Ideas: The Future of Policing and Human Rights

We live in a time of rapid social transformation that requires new ideas and ways of thinking about the world. As our social world experiences constant change, we need to reimagine what kind of world we want to create as we precariously push toward the future. Clearly, our current course of human progress teeters on the edge of civilizational collapse. If we are to survive as a human species, and if we are to continue human civilization as we know it, we must change direction. It starts with human rights, not as merely a concept, but a practice that permeates every aspect of social life.

What institutions today consistently practice human rights? Upon closer scrutiny, the practice of human rights remains largely absent in our society. From war to mass incarceration, and from healthcare to education, we live in a society where corporate profit above people remains the order of the day.

On both sides of the political spectrum, people increasingly sense that something is deeply wrong with this world. While some people can't quite put their finger on the matter, and while others find refuge in ideology, people almost instinctually feel that the world lost its way. We lost our way. What's more, most people feel powerless to change the direction of history and the course of their lives. As C. Wright Mills put it:

> Nowadays people often feel that their private lives are a series of traps. They sense that within their everyday worlds, they cannot overcome their troubles, and in this feeling, they are often quite correct. What ordinary people are directly aware of and what they try to do are bounded by the private orbits in which they live; their visions and their powers are limited to the close-up scenes of job, family, neighborhood; in other milieux, they move vicariously and remain spectators. And the more aware they become, however vaguely, of ambitions and of threats which transcend their immediate locales, the more trapped they seem to feel.

(1959)

If we feel trapped, it's largely due to our failures to utilize our own sense of agency to impart meaningful change in the world beyond our immediate environment. We have become spectators to the world, watching other, more powerful people shape the direction of history and, therefore, our lives. Most of us simply follow the scripts imposed upon us at birth, following social norms and patterns of behavior that keep the juggernaut of society steering out of our control.

As Martin Luther King dreams and John Lennon imagines, we can create a new social world in our image. We can create a world where all people celebrate life and liberty, dignity and equality, recognition and protection, travel and asylum, independent thought and consciousness, expression and association, work and security, leisure and peace, health and well-being, education and enlightenment, culture and artistic/intellectual pursuits, and community and love. Can you too dream? Can you too imagine? If so, we can create such a world.

As the great Bob Dylan once said, "the times they are a-changin'," and it's up to us as the people to decide how our times will change—or it will be decided for us. Dylan also said, "He not busy being born is busy dying." Realizing our sense of agency is our existential rebirth, and our only hope to shape the world beyond the private orbit of our lives. As the philosopher Allen Watts says: "You're under no obligation to be the same person you were five minutes ago." We have agency. We possess the ability to transform society in ways that reflect the interests of our brothers and sisters in the global human community. We have one last chance to shape the world, reclaim our society, and usher in an era where human rights exist in every sphere of social life.

Practicing human rights in every aspect of life is the only path forward toward developing a "civilized" civilization and creating a healthy society. If we really want to make a difference, the path forward is clear.

Suggested Assignment

Applying Human Rights to Police Work

For this discussion board, use concepts and ideas discussed in this book (understanding and interpretations of human rights, applying the three types of human rights police social interactions, understanding the relationship between power and human rights, using human agency to advance human rights policing, understanding the relationship between storytelling and human rights, learning from interviews with community members, as a few examples) to apply human rights to your police interactions with the members of the community you police, protect, and serve. In particular, write three stories discussing how you used the ideas and concepts of this book to apply human rights to your police work. Please choose specific human rights from the Declaration of Human Rights or the International Covenant on Civil and Political Rights to showcase the rights you allowed or prevented community members from enjoying during your police interactions with members of the community. These stories can be of any length, but enough to provide a full and accurate detailed picture of what transpired during your policing interactions. In your discussion, please include in each story ways that you honored, or allowed individual community members to enjoy the human rights that belong to them throughout your policing interaction. What's more, please give your reasons for allowing or temporarily preventing community members from enjoying their human rights during the course of your interactions. Again, please make sure to show how you consciously applied the thoughts and ideas of the class to make human rights policing a reality.

Notes

1 At the time of this writing, US Border Patrol agents on horses used whips against black Haitian migrants on the Mexican-United States border.
2 See: www.youtube.com/watch?v=bntsfiAXMEE
3 See: Johnson, Jake. "House Approves $778 Billion Military Budget." December 8, 2021. *Scheerpost*.
4 See: Mohammed Hussein and Mohammed Hadded. "Infographic: US military presence around the world." *Aljazeera*. September 10, 2021. See also: Guyer, Jonathan. "Why the US is paying more for the military after the Afghanistan war is over." *Vox*. December 22, 2021.
5 See: www.atlasofplaces.com/essays/letters-from-the-earth/
6 See: www.wwf.org.uk/sites/default/files/2018-10/wwfintl_livingplanet_full.pdf
7 See: www.businessinsider.com/nixon-adviser-ehrlichman-anti-left-anti-black-war-on-drugs-2019-7
8 See: www.globalgiving.org/learn/how-much-would-it-cost-to-end-homelessness-in-america/
9 ALEC is an organization composed of powerful corporations that heavily influence social policy and elections; even further, they literally hand bills to congress members that turn into laws. According to its website, ALEX is "America's largest nonpartisan, voluntary membership organization of state legislators dedicated to the principles of limited government, free markets and federalism. Comprised of nearly one-quarter of the country's state legislators and stakeholders from across the policy spectrum, ALEC members represent more than 60 million Americans and provide jobs to more than 30 million people in the United States." See: https://alec.org/about/.
10 See: www.aclu.org/issues/criminal-law-reform/reforming-police/asset-forfeiture-abuse.
11 See: www.npr.org/2021/10/18/1047085626/supreme-court-police-qualified-immunity-cases
12 Ibid.
13 Ibid.

References

Arendt, Hannah. 1963. *Eichmann in Jerusalem: A Report on the Banality of Evil*. New York: Viking Press.

Arendt, Hannah. 1978. *The Life of the Mind: Thinking*, ed. Mary McCarthy. London: Secker & Warburg.

Butler, Smedley. 2018. *War is a Racket: original edition*. [Place of publication not identified]: Dauphine Publications.

Clarke, John, Stuart Hall, Tony Jefferson, and Brian Roberts. 1976. "Subcultures, Cultures, and Class." In *Resistance Through Rituals: Youth Subcultures in Post-War Britain*, edited by Stuart Hall and Tony Jefferson. London: Hutchinson, 3–59.

Churchill, Ward. 2003. *On the Justice of Roosting Chickens: Reflections on the Consequences of U. S. Imperial Arrogance and Criminality*. Chico, CA: AK Press.

Johnson, Jake. 2021. "House Approves $778 Billion Military Budget." December 8. Scheerpost.

Mills, C. Wright. 2000. *The Sociological Imagination*. Oxford, UK: Oxford University Press.

Mohammed, Hussein and Mohammed Hadded. 2021. "Infographic: US military presence around the world." Aljazeera. September 10.

Simmel, Georg. 1903. "The Metropolis and Mental Life." In *The Blackwell City Reader*, edited by Gary Bridge and Sophie Watson. Oxford and Malden, MA: Wiley-Blackwell, 2002, 11–19.

WWF. 2018. Living Planet Report—2018: Aiming Higher. Grooten, M. and Almond, R.E.A. (Eds). Gland, Switzerland: WWF, Gland.

Young, Jock. 2012. *The Criminological Imagination*. Cambridge: Polity.

Index

.

For Product Safety Concerns and Information please contact our EU
representative GPSR@taylorandfrancis.com
Taylor & Francis Verlag GmbH, Kaufingerstraße 24, 80331 München, Germany

www.ingramcontent.com/pod-product-compliance
Lightning Source LLC
Chambersburg PA
CBHW080134270326
41926CB00021B/4477